Trends in Contemporary Indian Philosophy of Education

A Critical Evaluation

G. Ranjit Sharma

ATLANTIC
PUBLISHERS & DISTRIBUTORS (P) LTD

Published by

ATLANTIC

PUBLISHERS & DISTRIBUTORS (P) LTD

7/22, Ansari Road, Darya Ganj, New Delhi-110002
Phones : +91-11-40775252, 40775214, 23273880, 23275880
Fax: +91-11-23285873
Web: www.atlanticbooks.com
E-mail: orders@atlanticbooks.com

Disclaimer-

- The author and the publisher have taken every effort to the maximum of their skill, expertise and knowledge to provide correct material in the book. Even then if some mistakes persist in the content of the book, the publisher does not take responsibility for the same. The publisher shall have no liability to any person or entity with respect to any loss or damage caused, or alleged to have been caused directly or indirectly, by the information contained in this book.
- The author has fully tried to follow the copyright law. However, if any work is found to be similar, it is unintentional and the same should not be used as defamatory or to file legal suit against the author.
- If the readers find any mistakes, we shall be grateful to them for pointing out those to us so that these can be corrected in the next edition.
- All disputes are subject to the jurisdiction of Delhi courts only.

Printed & bound in India by Atlantic Print Services

In Memory of

Contemporary Indian Thinkers

and

of Two Great Souls

—G.R. Sharma

Foreword

Most of the researches taken up in Indian universities in the last few decades have been concerned with western philosophy or ancient Indian philosophical systems. In the last two decades, however, scholars have started working in contemporary Indian philosophy. Initially most of the research works were concerned with some one of the contemporary Indian philosophers. Thus, researches were carried on the philosophy of Swami Vivekananda, Sri Aurobindo, Swami Dayananda, M.K. Gandhi, R.N. Tagore and S. Radhakrishnan among others. Again, most of the early researches concerned with metaphysical problems. It is only very recently that researches have been undertaken in the fields concerning practical application of philosophy, social philosophy, philosophy of education, philosophy of law, political philosophy, moral philosophy, philosophy of culture, etc. These researches have gathered valuable material of much practical importance and even advanced useful suggestions for solving practical problems in different fields. By the very nature of the case, a thesis propounds a theory. However, since every practical effort requires a theoretical foundation, theoretical research has been usefully utilized in various fields of life.

For good or for bad, economic viability has now become an important criterion in the field of knowledge. Every discipline is expected to contribute its mite to general national development. And philosophy is no exception to this rule. If the teachers and researchers in the field of philosophy awaken to this timely need philosophy may survive in Indian universities and colleges, as it is serving and progressing in countries like U.S.A. If this call of the time is not responded philosophy will attract very few students and researchers and even those who are attracted to it will not find warm reception in the world around them. Therefore, more and more philosophical researches should be conducted in the practical fields applying philosophy. It should be remembered here that skilled use of philosophical method in the fields of practical knowledge requires as much training in philosophical method as required by any scientist in the use of scientific method in any branch of science. Forgetting these fact scholars in various subjects like education, law, sociology, economics, etc., have committed grave mistakes by arriving at philosophical conclusions without adequate use of the philosophical methods. Principles have been confused with philosophy and one finds principles of sociology under the title of social philosophy and principles of education under the title of philosophy of education.

Keeping the above facts in mind most of the researches in philosophy at Meerut University have been concerned with areas of practical philosophy such as philosophy of education, political philosophy and social philosophy, etc. The author of this work Dr. G.R. Sharma decided to find out trends in Contemporary Indian Philosophy of Education. The trends not only highlight the preferences but also universal needs of the time. The conclusions reached by contemporary Indian philosophers of education are not only personal views but expressions of the needs of the time. Contemporary Indian thinkers were born at a time when the nation was passing through all types of travails, including those created by the foreign rule. These thinkers were the spokesmen of the national consciousness. They were not only men well-versed in contemporary knowledge but they fully imbibed ancient Indian cultural heritage. Their thought was a meeting ground of East and West, Ancient as well as Modern. This was very much reflected in the field of education. The conclusions reached by Dr. G.R. Sharma in his last Chapter not only admirably sum up areas of agreement in the fields of education but also unravel valuable recommendations made by these thinkers. The planners for new education must pay attention to these agreements and recommendations if the future schemes of education wish to deliver real goods.

By his laborious collection of the educational views of contemporary Indian philosophers of education Dr. G.R. Sharma has presented an admirable and systematic exposition. By his analysis of the trends he has predicted about the future and given valuable direction to planners in the field of education. By his critical evaluation he has shown what is dead and what is living in contemporary Indian philosophy. And last but not the least valuable is his scheme of an ideal philosophy of education for today in the concluding Chapter of his work. This work was very much appreciated by his examiners both concerning its contents as well as language. The author has been lucky that his work is being published within such a short time after its assessment. In fact, this reflects the appreciation of the quality of his work. The work is bound to evoke interest not only among teachers of philosophy and education but also among the researchers, the administrators and the planners in the field of education. It is a pleasure to write a foreword for such a work.

Dr. R.N. Sharma,
Chairman,
U.P. Philosophers Association

'Archana'
Civil Lines,
Meerut.

Preface

The present book is the Doctoral thesis of the author which was approved by the Meerut University for the degree of Doctor of Philosophy in the year 1985.

Behind the majority of the present problem of education in India is the absence of proper philosophical perspective. This philosophical perspective, while on the one hand, will include ancient Indian wisdom, it will also imbibe the results of Western experience in this field. Education today is a global problem. The national scheme of education must be consistent with a universal ideal of education. In order to find out philosophical basis for Indian education today one will have to go through a critical understanding and evaluation of the foremost among the contemporary Indian philosophers of education. These thinkers may be classified as revivalists or the neo-Vedantic philosophers on the one hand and those influenced by Western rationalism and humanism and other tendencies on the other. In the former class may be included Swami Vivekananda, Sri Aurobindo, Dayananda, M.K. Gandhi, Rabindra Nath Tagore and Sarvapalli Radhakrishnan. In the latter class the two leading names are M.N. Roy and Pandit J.L. Nehru. A critical evaluation and systematic understanding of the educational philosophy of these thinkers will unravel the philosophical basis required for the present day education, particularly about aims of education, means of education, types of education, medium of education, teaching methods and education for different sections of society. It will unravel the trends underlying the whole panorama of contemporary Indian philosophy of education. A critical evaluation of these trends and the exploration of a philosophical basis is the main objective for the present research. The method followed is construction through criticism.

Thus, this project is both critical and constructive. It aims at building up a profile of a national philosophy of education by a synthesis of the salient features of the foremost contemporary Indian educational philosophers.

In the completion of this work in the present form the author owes to his supervisor Dr. R.N. Sharma. D. Phil., D. Lit., Head of the Department of P.G. Studies and Research, Meerut College, Meerut University, acknowledged as a scholar among philosophers and educationists. With his wide experience of guiding research in philosophy and education, Dr. R.N. Sharma's insight has been the guiding light to the author throughout the process. He was kind enough to find time for discussion and clarification of different issues and encouraging the author at the critical periods.

The author registers his profound thanks to the Government of Manipur for granting him study leave for undertaking the present research.

The author also presumes that it will not be out of context of Indian cultural pattern, if he expresses his sense of gratitude to his parents and parent-in-laws for their constant encouragement and inspiration he received during the work.

The author is grateful to M/s. Atlantic Publishers & Distributors, New Delhi-110027 for publishing the present book within a short period in spite of their other heavy commitments.

Last but not the least, the author adores to appreciate sacrifices of his loving wife, Dr. (Mrs) Nungshitombi Devi Adhikari, Lecturer in Home Science, Govt. G.P. Women's College, Imphal. Besides, he also places on record the hurdles faced by his little children, Gitanjali and Kananbala during the work of their daddy.

G.R. Sharma

Khongman Manzil,
Imphal-795001
Manipur, India

Contents

1
Introduction

Education in the East and West has always had its foundations in the metaphysical, epistemological and axiological outlook of the philosophers. As metaphysics, epistemology and axiology differed so differed the system of education. In India the philosophical traditions have continued since ancient times to the present day. Therefore, one finds agreement on the broad issues concerning educational practice between the ancient and modern thinkers. This is the foundation of contemporary Indian philosophy of education.

Need of Philosophical Basis of Education

All modern educationists hold the view that not only should the educator be equipped with knowledge of a variety of subjects, but also that he should have his own philosophy of education, without which he cannot efficiently solve the problems that face him in teaching from day-to-day. Fitches rightly said, "The art of education will never attain complete clearness in itself without philosophy. Hence, there is an interaction between the two, and either without the other is incomplete and unserviceable." Some people are so impressed by the achievements of science that they give a higher place to science than to philosophy in education. Psychologists are of the opinion that education should be based on psychological principles, while sociologists, impressed by the significance of social phenomena, suggest that education should be more influenced by their findings. But all these people forget that even sociologists and psychologists have failed to solve many difficulties that have arisen in connection with the aims of education, curriculum, teaching methods, discipline, etc. They have even failed to provide a satisfactory criterion for determining techniques of evaluation, standards of evaluation, selection of text books or of teaching methods. In actual fact, there is no rivalry between philosophy and science because philosophy gives adequate importance to the principles enunciated by psychology and sociology. The only real difference is that philosophy is concerned with more fundamental problems, that delves far more deeply than any one science, that its attitude is far more comprehensive and liberal and that it is an attempt at synthesizing most of the viewpoints from which any phenomenon is examined. Hence, the educator cannot do without philosophy.

The educator is often faced with the problems in the sphere of education which can be solved only on the basis of his conception of the universe. Every behaviour or action has its own principle. Hence educational behaviour, too, must have its own principle. This principle underlying all educational behaviour is derived from philosophy of education. It is only through a philosophy of education that one can determine the curriculum, the text books, the methods of teaching, methods and standards of evaluation, the methods of maintaining discipline, etc. Hence, the educator should study educational philosophy.

Education seeks to reform society. This reformation depends on the philosophy concerning the individual and society. "The educational system which we attempt to set up", said G.D.H. Cole, "must depend on the kind of society we mean to live in, on the qualities in men and women on which we set the highest value, and on the estimates which we make of the educability both of those who are endowed with the higher intellectual or aesthetic capacities and of ordinary people."[1] Philosophy of education is theoretical. The theory, however, aims at the guidance to practice. In the words of John Dewey, "Whenever philosophy has been taken seriously, it has always been assumed that it signified achieving a wisdom that would influence the conduct of life."[2] Idealism has been the most ancient and the most prominent school in philosophy. In the words of Adams,

"Idealism in one form or other permits the whole of the history of philosophy."[3] This idealism again has been the most fundamental theory underlying educational principles. In the words of Robert R. Rusk, "It bestows dignity and grandeur upon human life by emphasising the distinctiveness of man's nature, attributing to him powers, not possessed by animals, which issue in ideals—logical and aesthetic; it admits the existence of a Supreme Being; by its respect for human personality it provides the basis for democracy."[4]

The most fundamental question in the field of education is concerning its aim. This question raises queries about the nature of man and the possibility of its modification and transformation. Man's nature is very much concerned with his place in the cosmos. Therefore, the question of the aim of education is very much concerned with the question of the nature of the universe. Again, it is intimately concerned with the concept of culture prevalent in a society. This makes for the close relation between philosophy and education. In the words of Blanshard and others, "The function of philosophy in universities is properly the same as its function in the cultural development of a society to be the intellectual conscience of the community."[5] Education is based upon the distinctions between animal and human nature. It has generally aimed to develop the characteristics peculiar to man. In the words of Robert R. Rusk, "Those powers and their products are peculiar to man, and differentiate him from other animals. They lie beyond the range of the positive science—biological and even psychological; they raise problems which only philosophy can hope to solve and make the only satisfactory basis of education a philosophical one."[6]

Education aims at imparting knowledge. Knowledge, however, requires a global outlook and a synthesis of various types of information and experiences. This is a philosophical activity without which no education is possible. Therefore, the need of philosophical basis of education is rooted in the branch of philosophy known as epistemology. As Aristotle has said, "Whether we philosophise or not, we must philosophise." This has been expressed by Perry in somewhat different terms when he says, "Philosophy is neither accidental nor supernatural, but inevitable and normal."[7] Besides its synthetic function, another important function of philosophy is the criticism of the postulates and conclusions of different sciences. Whenever a scientist delves deeper in his own particular field, he reaches a depth where the process of his thinking is not scientific but philosophical. This can be seen in the thinking of many a great scientists of the world. The importance of philosophy in the field of knowledge is, therefore, quite clear. From the point of view of different aspects of the individual and social life, and in different fields of knowledge, the discussion of the value of philosophy shows the utility of its study. In the words of J.W. Cunningham, "Philosophy thus grows directly out of life and its needs. Everyone who lives, if he lives at all reflectively, is in some degree a philosopher."[8] In the words of Chestertun, "The most practical and important thing about a man is his view of universe—his philosophy."[9]

Meaning of Philosophy

The above discussion of the need of philosophical basis of education will be more clear by an analysis of the meaning of philosophy. Meaning of a subject means what it stands for. It includes its definition, nature, scope and importance both in historical and literal perspectives. The meaning of philosophy has been a controversial matter since ancient times. Different philosophers defined philosophy from their own view points. A beginner in philosophy is perturbed to find that different philosophers have given different definitions of philosophy. While some philosophers have laid emphasis on psychological facts, others have given more importance to values. According to John Dewey, "Whenever philosophy has been taken seriously, it has always been assumed that it signified achieving a wisdom that would influence the conduct of life."[10] On the other hand, according to Windelband, philosophy is " . . . the critical science of universal values." While there is much difference in Indian and Western definitions of philosophy, one finds widely different definitions presented by Western philosophers also. Of these definitions some emphasise the critical aspects of philosophy while others lay emphasis upon its synthetic aspect. Some examples of these two types of definitions of philosophy are as follows:

(a) Philosophy is a critical method of approaching experience. Examples of this type of definitions are as follows:—

1. "Philosophy is essentially a spirit or method of approaching experience rather than a body of conclusions about experience."[11]
2. "It is not the specific content of these conclusions, but the spirit and method by which they are reached, which entitles them to be described as philosophical."[12]
3. "Were I limited to one line for my answer to it, I should say that philosophy is general theory of criticism."[13]

(b) Philosophy is comprehensive synthetic science. The following definitions of philosophy emphasize its synthetic aspect:—

1. "Philosophy, like science, consists of theories of insights arrived at as a result of systematic reflection."[14]
2. "Philosophy is concerned with everything as a universal science."[15]
3. "Our subject is a collection of sciences, such as theory of knowledge, logic, cosmology, ethics and aesthetics, as well as a unified survey."[16]

The above mentioned definitions of philosophy show that while some philosophers have mainly emphasized critical philosophy, others have defined it as a synthetic discipline. In fact both these viewpoints are one-sided because philosophy is both critical as well as synthetic. Literally speaking, the word "philosophy' involves two Greek words—*Philo* meaning love and *Sophia* meaning knowledge. Thus literally speaking, philosophy means love of wisdom. It should be noted here that this definition of philosophy is different from the sense in which the word *Darsan* has been taken in India. The literal meaning of philosophy shows that the philosopher is constantly and everywhere engaged in the search for truth. He does not bother so much to arrive at final conclusions and continues with his search for truth throughout his life. His aim is the pursuit of truth rather than its possession. Those who enjoy journey do not care so much about the destination, neither are they perturbed when the destination is lost in sight in spite of continued long journey.

In an effort to define philosophy, one arrives at the difficulty that there is no genus in this case and also no differentia. In defining a science one points out to the genus science and also to the particular area of the particular science which differentiates it from others. This is, however, not possible in the case of philosophy because philosophy is one and not many. Hence, in order to arrive at the meaning of philosophy we will have to discuss its problems, attitude, method, process, conclusions and results. In brief, philosophy is a philosophical process of solving some characteristic problems through characteristic methods, from a characteristic attitude and arriving at characteristic conclusions and results.[17] Some might find this definition very vague and inadequate. But while defining science, do we not say that science is scenting or that it is a method? And can we understand this definition of science without understanding scientific method? When science cannot be understood without knowing scientific method, how can we hope to understand philosophy without knowing philosophical method? Again, in understanding the definition of science we are required to understand not only scientific method but also scientific attitude, scientific process, scientific problems and scientific conclusions because all these together form a science. Therefore, what is vague and inadequate if we say that in order to understand philosophy one must understand the attitude, problems, activity, conclusions and results peculiar to it? This will also clarify the distinction between philosophy and science which has been forgotten by many philosophers.

Contemporary Indian philosophers have used the term philosophy almost in the same sense as it is used in the West. Thus, according to Sri Aurobindo, "the work of philosophy is to arrange the data given by the various means of knowledge, excluding none, and put them into synthetic relation to the one truth, the one supreme and universal Reality."[18] Philosophy should be all comprehensive, affirmative, synthetic and spiritual. Philosophy, as the Indians conceived it, is the knowledge of that by knowing which everything else can be known. Thus, philosophy is the knowledge of Ultimate Reality. But Ultimate Reality, as Indian philosophy truly maintains, is not only Existence but also Consciousness and Bliss. Hence, philosophy as the quest after ultimate truth, is science of value par excellence.[19] It should not only criticise facts but also satisfy human aspirations. It should synthesis value and existence, religion and science. To quote Sri Aurobindo, "It should be a discovery of the real reality of things by which human existence can learn its law and aim and the principle of its perfection."[20]

Meaning of Education in India and West

The word education has its origin in the Latin word '*educatum*' itself composed of two terms, 'E' and '*Duco*' 'E' implies a progress from inward to outward while '*Duco*' means developing or progressing. In its most literal sense, therefore, education means becoming developed or progressing from inside to outside. Education, thus, is the process of developing the inner abilities and powers of an individual. The term is also often connected with the Latin '*educere*', meaning a propulsion from the internal to the external. This Latin term means to educate through a change brought about by practice or usage. In this manner, education implies some kind of change for the better in person.

In general usage, the term education is used either in its narrow sense or in its more liberal connotation. A slight elaboration of these two senses is given here.

A large majority of people use the term to mean the training or studies undertaken for a few years in some educational institutions. This is the restricted meaning of the term. It implies education provided according to a fixed curriculum by a particular set of people in a specific place. It does not necessarily provide any real knowledge, since the individual still has much to learn. The qualities an individual needs to achieve success in practical life cannot be generated in him by college education. This meaning of the term pertains to the most formal kind of education, in which an individual pursues a course of study dictated by a standard curriculum and at the end of a stipulated period, wins a degree or diploma. This certificate enables him to get some kind of job. In actual fact, an individual should not be considered educated merely because he possesses a degree, while on the other hand, absence of such a degree should not imply that the individual is uneducated. In every country, there are instances of great social reformers, saints, philosophers and thinkers who have never been near an institution of formal education. But can they be called uneducated on this ground?

When the word is accepted in its more liberal meaning, it is granted that at all times and places an individual is imbibing some education. Education is thus not limited merely to the classroom. It can be obtained from all individuals, even from Nature. Considered from this standpoint, it can be said that the child gets education not only from his teacher but also from the entire complexity of his environment, each object in which is a means of educating him. It must be granted that, with this definition, the subjects of education cannot be determined, for they are far too numerous. Education is, therefore, also not limited to students but comprehends all human individuals, of all sizes and ages, races and groups.

In this sense, education is informal. Besides, this aspect of education has great importance. Such an education is not planned or organised. The child learns many new and interesting things from his parents, his friends at play, his neighbours and other members of society. Many things he can learn merely by observing others. It should not be concluded from this description that the restricted and the liberal, or the formal and the informal implications of education are mutually exclusive. In actual fact, the term education is used in both these senses. Education in both its forms is essential for a complete development of the individual. An individual who is formally educated is not necessarily completely developed, but he is unquestionably better informed than the average uneducated person. Besides, he develops the ability to imbibe education, as it is meant in its more liberal sense. Education of both kinds is, thus, essential.

Meaning of Education in the West

Educational thinking, like every other branch of knowledge, started in the philosophical deliberation of the ancient Greek philosophers. Thus, the meaning of education in West is initially available in the works of Plato. It is interesting to note that thousands of years ago Plato gave a meaning to education which is even now followed in the West with slight changes here and there. Plato defined education as a lifelong process starting, "From the first years of childhood and lasting to the very end of the life."[21] He used the term education in a very wide sense, "Which makes a man eagerly pursue the ideal perfection of citizenship and teaches him how rightly to rule and how to obey."[22] Education not only provides knowledge and skills but also inculcates values, training of instincts, fostering right attitudes and habits. In *Republic,* Plato points out, "that true education, whatever that may be, will have the greatest tendency to civilise and humanise them in their relation to another and to those who are under their protection."[23] This humanist definition of education propounded by Plato is still the most widely accepted meaning of education in the West. Education everywhere has been used as a process of inculcating values. As Plato said, "Now I mean by education that training which is given by suitable habits to the first instincts of virtue in children."[24] These views of Plato have been universally accepted in the West as well as in the East. Education has been defined differently by the idealists, the pragmatists, the naturalists and the realist philosophers. However, its meaning has been generally idealistic. Without some sort of idealism there can be no education worth the name. In the words of Robert R. Rusk, "We may accept that the aim of education is the enhancement or enrichment of personality, the differentiating feature of which is the embodiment of universal values."[25] The western educational philosophers have generally agreed that free growth of the human child is the essence of education. In the words of A.G. Hughes, "The essence of discipline is, thus not forced subordination to the will of hated tyrants, but submission to the example of admired superiors."[26] In the middle ages Comenius declared education to be a process whereby an individual developed qualities relating to religion, knowledge and morality, and thereby established his claim to be called a human being. "The fundamental principles of education", according to Froebel, "instruction and teaching should be passive and protective not directive and interfering."[27] The principles of liberty has found most eloquent expression in the definition of education given by Rousseau when he said, "Let us obey the call of Nature. We shall see that her yoke is easy and that when we give heed to her voice we find the joy in the answer of a good conscience."[28] Others have laid emphasis upon the social meaning of education whereby it aims at making an individual fit in the society. It was in this sense that Aldous Huxley said, "A perfect education is one which trains up every human being to fit into the place he or she is to occupy in the social hierarchy, but without, in the process, destroying his or her individuality."[29]

All the foregoing definitions have stated that education is the process of development. It, therefore, becomes necessary to discover what is implied in this development. Although the ability to learn depends upon development, but development is not synonymous with education. Development means the gradual and continuous progress of mind and body. Through this development the child acquires the following elements:

1. Knowledge of the environment by which he is surrounded.
2. The necessary motor control to fulfill his individual needs.
3. Some knowledge of individual and collective relationships.
4. Linguistic abilities to enable him to converse.

The development of all these elements begins at home itself. The educator's task is to continue this process and to encourage it while the child is at school.

In fact this process of development continues right through an individual's lifetime. Consequently, it is accepted that education in its general sense continues throughout a man's natural span of life. Even the successful teacher or educator himself remains a student through his life. On the one hand he teaches certain things to some people but at the same time he learns something from them. All successful educators experience that the development undergone by this thoughts, personalities and abilities would have been impossible otherwise. In much the same way, people other than the educators, teach and learn simultaneously.

Meaning of Education in India

Turning to the Indian approach, it becomes necessary to include the spiritual aspect also because it is accepted as a part of the development by education. In fact, Indian thinkers have special emphasis upon this. Yajnavalkya opined that only that is education which gives a sterling character to an individual and renders him useful for the world. Sankaracarya maintained that education is that which leads to salvation. Even the more recent educationists, some of whose ideas are expressed below, have stressed the importance of the spiritual aspect. In the words of A.S. Altekar, "Education has always been regarded in India as a source of illumination and power which transforms and ennobles our nature by the progressive and harmonious development of our physical, mental, intellectual and spiritual powers and faculties."[30]

This spiritual tradition has been carried on by contemporary Indian philosophers of education in their integral approach, synthesis of idealism and pragmatism, rationalism and humanism, diversity in unity and harmony of the individual and society. It was due to this emphasis on the spiritual meaning of education that Swami Vivekananda said, "Religion is the inner most core of education."[31] In the words of Sri Aurobindo, "The child's education ought to be an out bringing of all that is best, most powerful, most intimate and living in his nature, the mould into which the man's action and development ought to run is that of his innate quality and power. He must acquire new things but he will acquire them best, most wholly on the basis of his own developed type and inborn force."[32] M.K. Gandhi expressed the same idea when he defined education by saying, "By education I mean an all round drawing out of the best in child and man, body, mind and spirit. Literacy is not the end of education not even the beginning. It is one of the means whereby man and woman can be educated. Literacy in itself is no education."[33]

Synthetic Definition

It is clear from the above discussion of the meaning of education in West and India, ancient and modern that they may be synthesised since all these accept some common characteristics of education. The following points concerning the meaning of education emerge from a review of the meaning of education in the West and in India:

1. *A lifelong process*: Education according to most of the philosophers continues from birth to death. As Madan Paul

Richard pointed out, the education of man, "should begin at his very birth and it is to continue the whole of life."[34]

2. ***Unfolding***: Education is a gradual unfolding. In his allegory of the cave, Plato observes, "that the power and capacity of learning exists in the soul already, and just as the eye was unable to turn from darkness to light, without the whole body, so too, the instrument of knowledge can only, by the movement of the whole soul, be turned from the world of becoming into that of being and learn by degrees to endure the sight of being and of the brightest and best of being or in other words of the good."[35] It is in the same sense that Sri Aurobindo said, "The chief aim of education should be to help the growing soul to draw out that in itself which is best and make it perfect for a noble use."[36]

3. ***Based on child psychology***: Western thinkers unanimously agreed that true education should be based on child psychology. This again has been accepted by Indian philosophers of education. According to Sri Aurobindo, "Nothing can be taught to the mind which is not already concealed as potential knowledge in the unfolding soul of the creature."[37] Educational theory must be based on sound psychology. As Sri Aurobindo points out, "The true basis of education is the study of the human-mind, infant, adolescent and adult."[38]

4. ***Individual as well as social***: True education is individual as well as social. Plato brought out a scheme of education-according to each individual's capacities to serve the society. Philosophers in the West have everywhere laid emphasis upon individual as well as social aims of education. Contemporary Indian philosophers also exhibit this tendency. M.K. Gandhi said, "I value individual freedom, but you must not forget that man is essentially a social being. He has risen to his present status by learning to adjust his individuality to the requirements of social progress."[39]

5. ***Total development***: Thus education by general agreement is a total development, physical, mental and spiritual, individual as well as social. This total development is the meaning of self-realisation. As J.M. Baldwin commented, "The real self is the bipolar self." This synthesis of the different aspects of man's development is characteristic of not only idealism but also naturalism, pragmatism and realism. It is again the meaning of perfection, acclaimed as the aim of education by so many

thinkers. It is also what is known as complete education. It is again the humanist meaning of education since man is a complex being having several aspects of his personality all of which require full development. According to Sri Aurobindo education should help the individual to grow, "into a fullness, of physical and vital energy and utmost breath, depth and height of his emotional, his intellectual and his spiritual being."[40] The total development lays equal emphasis upon physical as well as spiritual growth. Without physical culture mental training has been considered as one sided. In the words of Aldus Huxley, "Where the body is maladjusted and under strain, the mind's relations, sensory, emotional, intellectual, cognitive, with external reality are likely to be unsatisfactory."[41]' Education aims at an all round and total perfection of the individual and society. Hence, physical culture should form an important part of the educational process. As Sri Aurobindo puts it, "If seeking is for a total perfection of the being, the physical part of it cannot be left aside, for the body is the material basis, the body is the instrument which we have to use."[42] Similar quotations may be hunted from other philosophers of education in West and East. The total development involves character development, development of social virtues and individual skills. It includes all the various aims of education. It involves all the functions of education in human life such as development of natural abilities, character building, personality integration, preparation for adult life, control and sublimation of basic instincts, education for useful citizenship, development of a sense of community, progress of culture and civilization, social welfare, use of leisure and the synthesis of national as well as international consciousness.

Value of Indigenous Philosophy of Education

The synthetic definition of education will be, however, put into practice according to indigenous philosophy of education. That is the requirement for a scheme of rational system of education. Though philosophy is universal, each society in the world has developed a national philosophy characteristic of the thinking of a particular society through the ages. Thus, one finds significant and developmental differences not only in the philosophy of East and the philosophy of West but also in the philosophical systems of India, China, Japan, Iran and all other Asian countries. This is so since philosophical reflection does not act in a vacuum but is very much influenced by ecology, natural as well as social. Philosophy influences not only the world view but also the political, social, economic, religious, cultural and spiritual life of a nation. For example, the political history in India is very much different from the political history of U.S.A. Therefore, it will not be wise to apply results of experiments in American political life to Indian situation without any distinction. It is hence that indigenous philosophy of education is the only sound basis for educational reconstruction in a country. In the words of Blanchard and others, "The function of philosophy in universities is properly the same as its function in the cultural development of a society, to be the intellectual conscience of the community."[43]

Indian philosophy of education is rooted in Indian culture. The basic characteristic of Indian culture is an integral approach to life. Therefore, only an integral philosophy of education can suit Indian society. Indian philosophers have interpreted human nature as essentially good and divine. They have considered liberation as the goal of life. To them spiritual level is the highest level of development. The microcosm and macrocosm have been interpreted identically. In human nature itself the Indian psychologist has always kept his eye on totality including physical, vital, mental, physical and spiritual aspects. He has always aimed at integral personality. Indian philosophy of education is a happy synthesis of idealism and pragmatism. While laying emphasis upon the cosmic, the universal and the total truth and reality, Indian thinkers have recognised the value of plurality, multiplicity and individuality as equally important expressions of the ultimate reality. Therefore, a philosophy of education integral in aims, curriculum, psychology, practice, teaching methods and means of education will alone suit Indian society. Such a philosophy of education has been advanced in contemporary times by Swami Vivekananda, Sri Aurobindo, Swami Dayananda, M.K. Gandhi, Rabindra Nath Tagore, Sarvapalli Radhakrishnan, J.L. Nehru and M.N. Roy. Of these the first six belong to ancient Indian tradition and the next two are impressed by modern Western thinking. However, all these are humanist nationalists and aim at educational regeneration of Indian society. Therefore, the fundamental characteristics of educational thinking of contemporary philosophers of education will be the only proper basis for a national system.

References

1. Cole, G.D.H., *Essays in Social Theory* (London: Macmillan & Co., 1950), p. 47.
2. Dewey, J., *Democracy and Education* (New York : The Macmillan Co., 1916), p. 378.
3. Adams, Sir John, *The Evolution of Educational Theory* (Macmillan & Co., 1912), p. 28.
4. Rusk, R.R., *The Philosophical Bases of Education* (London University of London Press, 1956), p. 154.
5. Blanshard and others, *Philosophy in American Education* (New York: Harper & Bros., 1945), p. 80.
6. Rusk, R.R., *op. cit.*, p. 154.
7. Perry, *The Approach to Philosophy*, p. 22.
8. Cunningham, J.W., *Problems of Philosophy* (Calcutta: Chakarvarty, Chatterjee & Co., 1957), p. 5.
9. Quoted by Hocking, *Types of Philosophy*, p. 4.
10. Dewey, J., *Democracy and Education* (New York: The Macmillan Co., 1916), p. 378.
11. Brightman, E.S., *Introduction to Philosophy* (New York: Henery Holt & Co., 1925), p. 9.
12. Barret, C., *Philosophy* (New York: The Macmillan Co., 1935), p. 5.
13. Ducasse, C.J., *Philosophy of Art* (New York: Dial Press, 1926), p. 3.
14. Leighton, J.A., *The Field of Philosophy* (New York: Appleton Century Crofts, 1910), p. 4.
15. Quoted by R.N. Sharma, *Problems of Philosophy* (Meerut: Kedar Nath Ram Nath, 1982), p. 5.
16. Sellers, R.W., *The Principles and Problems of Philosophy* (New York : The Macmillan Co., 1926), p. 3.
17. Sharma, R.N., *Problems of Philosophy*, p. 6.
18. Aurobindo, S., *The Renaissance in India* (Pondicherry: Sri Aurobindo Ashram, 1951), p. 72.
19. Maitra, S.K., *Sri Aurobindo Mandir Annual*, Vol. II. p. 61.
20. Aurobindo, S., *The Human Cycle* (New York : The Sri Aurobindo Ashram Library, Inc., (1950), p. 93.

21. Plato, *Protagoras*, Jowett, 325.
22. Plato, *Laws,* Jowett, 644.
23. Plato, *Republic*, Jowett, 416.
24. Plato, *Laws*, Jowett, 653.
25. Rusk, R.R., *The Philosophical Bases of Education* (London University of London Press, 1956), p. 154.
26. Hughes, A.G., *Education and the Democratic Ideal* (London: Longman's Green & Co., 1951), p. 92.
27. Froebel's *Chief Educational Writings on Education* Translated by Dr. Fletcher, p. 32.
28. Rousseau, J.J., *Emile* (London: J.M. Dent & Sons, 1950), p. 251.
29. Huxley, A *Proper Studies* (London: Chatto and Windus, 1928), p. 136.
30. Altekar, A.S., *Education in Ancient India* (Banaras: The Indian Book Shop, 1934), p. 8.
31. Vivekananda, S., *The Complete Works* (C.W.), (Calcutta: Advaita Ashrama), Vol. 5, p. 161.
32. Aurobindo, S., *Essays on the Gita* (Calcutta: Arya Publishing House, 1949), p. 319.
33. Gandhi, M.K., *Harijan*, 31-7-1937.
34. *Sri Aurobindo and the Mother on Education* (Pondicherry: Sri Aurobindo Ashram, 1972), First edition, p. 59.
35. Plato, *Republic*, Jowett, 518.
36. Aurobindo, S., *A System of National Education* (Calcutta: Arya Publishing House, 1949), p. 5.
37. Aurobindo, S., *The Synthesis of Yoga* (New York: Sri Aurobindo Library Inc., 1950), p. 2.
38. Aurobindo, S., *A System of National Education* (Calcutta: Arya Publishing House, 1949), p. 1.
39. Gandhi, M.K., *Harijan*, 27-5-1939.
40. Aurobindo, S., *Birth Centenary Library*, Vol. 15, 1971, p. 605.
41. Huxley, A., *Ends and Means* (London: Chatto & Windus, 1951), p. 220.
42. Aurobindo, S., *The Supramental Manifestation* (Pondicherry: Sri Aurobindo Ashram, 1952), p. 8.
43. Blanshard and others, *Philosophy in American Education* (New York: Harper & Bros., 1945), p. 80.

2

Historical Review

History is a constant process though it is controversial whether it repeats itself. Various philosophers of history have shown various trends in historical process. Historical review in a particular area, however, shows the continuity of thought as well as the ancient origin of various ideas. This is particularly true in Indian context since contemporary Indian philosophers of education, Swami Vivekananda, Sri Aurobindo, Dayananda, M.K. Gandhi, Rabindra Nath Tagore and Sarvapalli Radhakrishnan, have presented ancient wine of wisdom in new bottles in the form of their philosophies of education. They openly swear by the ancient scriptures and develop their ideas on its foundations. They have only interpreted the old principles in the light of new knowledge and in the context of contemporary circumstances. Except M.N. Roy and J.L. Nehru all the contemporary Indian philosophers of education show the trends whose roots may be found in ancient Indian philosophy of education. The roots of the philosophy of education of J.L. Nehru and M.N. Roy may be traced to modern Western philosophy of education. Therefore, a historical review of ancient, medieval and modern philosophy of education is a prelude to the understanding of contemporary Indian philosophy of education. This has been attempted in this Chapter.

Ancient Indian Philosophy of Education

The pivot of the whole educational system of ancient India was the teacher variously called *acarya*, *guru, upadhyaya*. In *Manu* and other *smritis* there is some divergence about the greatness of the *acarya*. According to *Manusmriti*, the father (*janaka)* and the teacher are called father (*pita)* but the father who imparts the sacred *Veda* is superior to the father that gives birth, since the birth in spiritual learning is for a *brahmana*, of eternal benefit, here and hereafter.[1] But in another place Manu says that an *acarya* is ten times superior to an *upadhyaya*, the father is superior to a hundred *acaryas* while the mother is thousand-fold superior to the father.[2] According to Gautama, the *acarya* is the highest among all *gurus* while according to some the mother is the highest.[3] According to *Yajnavalkya Smriti* the mother is higher than the *acarya*.[4] The *Dharmasastras* define the *acarya* as one who performs the *upanayana* of the student and imparts the whole *Veda* to him.[5] The *Nirukta* defines *acarya* as follows: he makes the student understand the proper course of conduct, or he collects wealth from the student or gathers together the meanings of words, or he increases the intelligence of the student.[6] According to *Apastamba Dharma Sutra*, "The *acarya* is so called since the student gathers his duties from him."[7] According to *Manusmriti*, the teacher, after performing *upanayana*, teaches his pupil the rules about *sauca* (bodily purity), *acarya* (rules of conduct in everyday life), the offering (of fuel-stick) in fire and *sandhya* adoration.[8] Though the words *acarya*, *guru* and *upadhyaya* are very often used as synonyms, ancient writers made a distinction between them. According to *Manusmriti*, an *upadhyaya* is one who teaches to a student a portion of the *Veda* or the *Vedangas* (subsidiary lores of the *Veda)* as a means of his own livelihood and a *guru* is one who performs the *samskaras* and who maintains the child.[9] This latter definition shows that *guru* means the father here. According to *Yajnavalkya Smriti*, the *guru* is one who performs the *samskaras* and imparts the *Veda*.[10] This corroborates the statement made above that originally, the father himself taught the *Veda* to his son. The word *guru* is often used in the sense of any elderly person, male or female, who is entitled to respect. According to *Visnu Dharmasastra* the father, the mother and the *acarya* are the three highest *gurus* of a person.[11] According to *Manusmriti* whoever confers on another the benefit of knowledge, whether great or small, is the latter's *guru*.[12] All these praises of the *guru* by the *Dharmasastras* show that they held knowledge as the highest value and insisted upon the sense of gratitude in everyone who achieved knowledge. Faith in the teacher was a necessary qualification for the achievement of knowledge. It is undeniable that this glorification of the teacher may have led to some of them losing their heads but in contrast to the modern western philosophy of education, making the educand rather the educator the pivot of education it has its advantages. In fact both these extremes are unjust, the former to the educated and the latter to the educator. In a just system of education both should be given a proper place.

Qualification of the Educator

The *Dharmasastras* have not praised the teacher without any reason. They have insisted upon very high qualifications for being a teacher. They have warned about the dangers of entrusting the job of a teacher to persons not worthy of it. According to *Apastamba Dharma Sutra* he whom a teacher, devoid of learning, initiates, enters from darkness into darkness and he also (an *acarya)* who is himself unlearned (enters into darkness).[13] It further provides that one should desire a performer of one's *upanayana* who is endowed with learning and whose family is hereditarily learned and who is serene in mind and that one should study *Vedic* lore under him upon the end (of *brahmacarya)* as long as the teacher does not fall off from the path of *dharma.*[14] Similar qualifications have been laid down by other *Dharmasastras*. The teacher had to be a *brahmana*, learned in *Vedas*, knowing *Dharma*, pure, coming from good family and having an ideal character. In education system also the *Dharmasastras* have insisted upon the *varna* hierarchy. It has been generally maintained that *Brahmana* should be the teacher. According to *Vayupurana*, as to the *acarya* in *upanayana* must be a *brahmana*, as to the study of *Veda* one should ordinarily learn the *Veda* from a *Brahmana* teacher; in times of difficulty (i.e. when a *Brahmana* is not available) one may learn the *Veda* from *Kshatriya* or *Vaisya* teacher; but in such circumstances the only service that a *Brahmana* student rendered to the *guru* would be following after the *non-Brahmana* teacher; he had not to render bodily services (such as shampooing or washing the feet, etc.).[15] The *Mitaksara* on *Yajnavalkya Smriti* remarks that a *Kshatriya* or *Vaisya* should teach a *Brahmana* only when urged by him and not at his sweet will. Manu allowed only teaching to a *Kshatriya*, but did not allow him to make it a means of his livelihood. In fact the Indian thinkers prescribed a social structure with definite division of labour and permitted only exceptions in certain cases. They very much insisted upon keeping the social structure in tact and not violating it. This rigidity had obviously resulted in so many disadvantages but it also facilitated continuity, regularity and order in social system.

The Educand

The method of instruction of education was generally oral. The first thing that was taught to the boy was the *pranava* and *vyartis* and the *Gayatri*. Then the boy was to be taught other parts of the *Veda*. Detailed instructions were laid down about the method of teaching. According to *Manusmriti*, the student should sip water *(acamana)* when about to begin Vedic study, should face the north, should fold both hands together (and place them on his knee), should wear light (pure) clothes, should at the beginning and end of Vedic study clasp the feet of the teacher with crossed hands and should touch the right foot of the teacher with his own right hand and left foot with the left hand, should repeat '*om*' at the beginning of the Vedic study. The teacher should say to the pupil 'repeat' and should stop from teaching with the words 'let there be a pause.'[16] The study of the *Veda* was the first duty of every twice born person (*dvijati*). According to *Manusmriti*, all the *Vedas*, together with *Upanisads*, were to be learnt by every *dvijati*,[17] According to *Yajnavalkya Smriti*, it is *Veda* alone that confers the highest bliss upon *dvijatis* by enabling them to understand and perform sacrifices, austerities and auspicious acts (like *samskaras)*.[18] Since the literature was very wide concessions had to be made to the shortness of human life and the weakness of the human mind. Therefore, generally it was prescribed that one should study the *sakha* of the *Veda* which his ancestors' studied and should perform religious rites according to it. As the study of the *Veda* was a duty enjoined upon a *Brahmana*, so teaching *Veda* to another was a duty. This exclusive glorification of the *Brahmins* very much led to what

N.K. Dutt describes as the "price of scholasticism" among the professed scholars.[19] And it has been rightly pointed out by S. Cromwell Crawford, "Compounded with racial and sacerdotal pride, the pride of scholasticism elevated barriers between *Brahmins* and *non-Brahmins*."[20] In this way the good effect of the strictness of *Brahmacarya* in specialising learning and in enforcing high moral discipline was neutralised by the increased-rigidness and hauteur of caste, which is one of the many factors making India a land of contrasts.[21]

According to *Chhandogya Upanisad* the student had to serve the teacher by tending his cattle, had to beg for food and announce it to the teacher, and to look after his sacred fires and to learn the *Veda* only in the time that would be left after doing work for the *guru*.[22] Besides these, the rules concerning his conduct towards the teacher, the teacher's wife and son, concerning the method of salutation and showing respect, the food, drinks and actions allowed or prohibited to students are too numerous to be set out in detail. Both *Manusmriti* and *Yajnavalkya Smriti,* along with some other notable *Dharmasutras*, lay down the following rules for *Brahmacharin*. The student should speak the truth, bathe every day, should not look at the sun, should avoid honey, flesh, perfumes, the wearing of flowers, sleeping by day, rubbing oil on the body, putting collyrium in the eyes, going in a cart, wearing shoes and holding an umbrella, love affairs, anger, covetousness, infatuation, vain discussions, playing on musical instruments, luxurious baths with hot water, meticulous cleansing of the teeth, ecstatic states of mind, dancing, singing, calumny of others, dangerous places, gazing at woman or touching young woman, gambling, serving a low person (or doing very low work) injury to animals, obscene or harsh talk and wine. Manu prescribes that he should not sleep on a cot and should complete celibacy, but if he suffers from, night emissions he should bathe, worship the sun and repeat thrice the mantras '*punar mam*'[23] The *Apastamba Dharma Sutra* contains similar rules of conduct. According to it the student should not wash his limbs with hot water (generally), but he may do so if they are smeared with dirty and impure matter provided he does it out of the sight of the teacher and that he should not bathe in water in a sportive manner, but should bathe in it motionless like a stick.[24] It also not only prohibits him sexual intercourse but ordains that he should speak with women only as much as is absolutely necessary. The student was not to laugh, but if he could not help laughing he should do so covering his face with his hands.

According to Gautama and *Baudhayana Dharma Sutra* the student is to serve his teacher by following after him when he goes anywhere, he should help the teacher in his toilet and bath and should shampoo his body and take food left by him (*uccista*),[25] he should be diligent in doing work that would be pleasing and beneficial to the teacher; he was to study when the teacher called him, he was not to cover his throat with piece of cloth, or was not to sit in the presence of his teacher with his feet on his lap, was not to stretch his feet, he was not to clear loudly his throat nor to laugh, yawn or crack the knuckles; he was when called by the teacher to reply at once leaving his seat or had and was to approach the teacher even when he called from a distance; he should always occupy a seat lower than that of his teacher and should go to sleep after his teacher and rise before him. Similar rules have been prescribed by other *Dharmasastras*.[26] According to *Manusmriti* a pupil should not mimic the gait, the manner of speech and the actions of the teacher.[27] It calls upon the pupil to close his hands or fingers or to leave the place where somebody indulges in calumnies about the teacher or points out the faults in him, and states that if the pupil himself finds fault with his teacher or calumniates him, the pupil in the next life is born as an ass or a dog.[28] One of the rules for the student was that he was not to pronounce the name of his teacher even when the teacher was not present without prefixing or affixing an honorific addition such as *sri*, *bhatta*, *acarya*, etc. The student should not speak of his teacher, the teacher's son or wife or of a man who has been initiated for a *srauta* sacrifice by their bare names.[29] When it is absolutely necessary to refer to these by name the student should not pronounce the name and *gotra* of his teacher as they are, but by means of a synonym. According to *Apastamba Dharma Sutra*, even after returning home a *snataka* should avoid touching his former teacher with his fingers to call his attention, frequent muttering of something in his ears, laughing into his face, calling out loudly, taking his name, ordering him about.[30] According to *Manusmriti* a man who has been initiated for a *strauta* sacrifice should not be addressed by his name, even though he may be younger than the person addressing, but that one should use the '*bhoh*' and '*bhavat*' when addressing him or speaking about him and may refer to him by words like *diksita*, etc.[31] Very detailed rules were laid down about *pretathana* or rising from one's seat to receive a person, *abhivadana* or saluting a man, *upasamgrahana* or saluting by clasping the feet of the teacher or another with one's hands, *pratyabhivadana* or returning a salutation, and *namaskara* or bowing with the word namah. According to *Apastamba Dharma Sutra*, the student must clasp his teacher's feet when he meets his teacher after sunrise, and also beginning the day's lesson of Vedic study and even after finishing it. This has been corroborated by Manu.[32]

It should not be supposed that the *Dharmasastras*, while insisting upon educands "respect towards the educator, used less strict words while insisting educators' duty towards the educand." In fact the educational relationship was a two way relationship. It was reciprocal. According to *Apastamba Dharma Sutra*, "Loving him like his own son, and full of attention, he shall teach him the sacred science, without hiding anything in the whole law. And he shall not use him for his own purposes to the detriment of his studies, except in times of distress. The pupil who, attending to (teacher), accuses his (principal and first) teacher of ignorance, remains no (longer) a pupil. A teacher also, who neglects the instruction (of his pupil), does no (longer) remain a teacher."[33] The purport of education was the moral and intellectual growth of the students. These two elements were never separated. Indeed, the latter was contingent upon the former. According to the sacred law, only the person who is pure may be instructed in the *Veda*. Neither (the study of) the *Vedas*, nor liberality, nor sacrifices, nor any (self-imposed) restraint, nor austerities, ever procure the attainment (of rewards) to a man whose heart is contaminated (by sensuality).[34] "Moral culture not only preceded intellectual culture, but was the weightier of the two; A *Brahmana*, who completely governs himself, though he knows the *Savitri* only, is better than he who knows the three *Veda*, (but) does not control himself."[35]

The absence of social justice in education is particularly observed in the case of partially towards the education of all the *varnas* other than *Brahmin* and also of the women. These were given a secondary place. Literary education among women was in a languishing state. Therefore, there was no question of co-education. No much material is available about the education of *Ksatriyas*, *Vaisyas* and *Sudras*.. The entire education system was entrusted to *Brahmanas*. Summing up the state of education in *Dharmasastras,* P.V. Kane has written, "The salient features of the educational system outlined in the *Dharmasastra* works are the high and honourable position assigned to the teacher, the close personal contact of the pupil with the teacher and individual attention, the pupil's stay with the teacher as a member of his family, oral instruction and the absence of books, stern discipline and control of emotions and the will, cheapness, as no fees were stipulated for."[36]

The institution of education, as prescribed in ancient India can be favourably compared with any other system of education in the West, ancient or modern. Given the high character and scholarship of the teacher, it was the most ideal system of education. However, its defects are equally obvious. Summarising these defects, P.V. Kane has admitted, "The defects of the Indian system were that it was too literary, there was too much memorizing, boys under it had hardly any instruction in useful manual arts and crafts, the studies were not brought in contact with practical life. The discipline was rigorous and joyless. Many of these defects were due to the exigencies of the caste system which assigned particular avocations to particular castes."[37] Kane, however, rightly adds, "We cannot and should not compare the system with the systems of education prevalent in the 20th century, when several subjects such as literature, music and fine arts, handicrafts, mathematics, science, history and geography are taught in the schools to all boys and when it has been recognised that education is a prime concern of the State."[38]

Medieval Indian Philosophy of Education

Medieval Indian philosophy of education was developed by Muslims. The country in the north was generally under the reign of Muslim kings. In south India, however, and also in some other parts of the country Hindu kings ruled who perpetuated the ancient Indian philosophy of education in their educational institutions. The scheme of Muslim education flowed in India for a period of about five hundred years. This medieval period continued till the advent of British in India who started what is known as modern Indian philosophy of education which will be discussed in sequence.

The important features of Medieval Indian philosophy of education governed by Muslims were as follows: Muslim rulers took keen interest in the propagation of education since it had been appreciated by Muslim scriptures. The state provided aids to *Maktabs* and *Madarassas.* While the smaller *Maktabs* were regularly given financial aid, the bigger institutions were granted landed property for a permanent financial provision. The kings always gave status of eminence to scholars in their codes. Most of the *Madarassas* and *Maktabs* were connected with Mosques. Therefore, the institutions were mainly meant for Muslim students.

The media of education was Arabic and Persian. Only gradually Urdu developed, first in courts and then in educational institutions. In those parts of the country where Muslim kings ruled, the Hindu also used to learn Arabic and Persian languages since it was essential for securing employment in Government offices.

As explicit in the ancient Indian philosophy of education, the medieval Indian philosophy of education was also influenced by religion. It may be said that the modern secular education had its beginning in British period. Before that since ancient to modern times Indians always followed education as dictated by their religion. While the Hindus, particularly those living under Hindu Kingdoms, followed the philosophy of education advanced by Hindu scriptures, the Muslims followed the instructions of *Koran* in this connection. In *Maktabs* the first aim of education was to instill the basic tenets of Islam among the students. The students were required to memorise *Koran.* The *Maktabs* and *Madarassas* were instrumental for the propagation of Islamic ideas.

The medieval philosophy of education had two aims, one the propagation of the fundamental tenets and teachings of religion and the other to make the students practically successful in different vocations. The educational institutions, therefore, used to teach various arts and skills, such as sculptures, agriculture, medicine, painting, house building and various types of crafts. This was necessary for a regular supply of skilled and educated artisans and craftsmen. Military science formed an important part of curriculum everywhere since wars were usual phenomena. Therefore, weaponry was a specialised profession mostly taught by training apprentices by individual experts. Thus, education prepared for earning livelihood. Followers of different religions were instructed in the teachings of their own religion. While some examples of communal trends may be observed everywhere, examples of treating all religions with equal respect were also not rare. While some Muslim kings did try to propagate only Islamic teachings through education, other Muslim kings gave generous aids to Hindu *pathshalas* also. This shows the humanist trend in education, however, limited it may be. In line with ancient Indian philosophy of education, medieval Indian philosophy of education exhibited trends of humanism, pragmatism, utilitarianism, materialism, pluralism and democratic values.

In medieval times thousands of *Madarassas* provided education in literature, mathematics, philosophy and medicine, etc. The bigger institutions had huge libraries attached to them. Such an institution was established by Mahmood Gawan at Bidar. During the reign of Feroz, Jaupur was a prominent centre of Muslim education. Delhi had the famous *Nasaris Madarassa.*

The syllabi of medieval institutions included literature, grammar, logic, philosophy, mathematics, law, astrology, history, geography, agriculture, medicine, etc. The medium of instruction in Hindu institutions was Sanskrit or regional languages and in Muslim institutions Arabic and Parsi. Religious scriptures formed an important part of syllabi in the institutions of Muslims and Hindus.

The method of teaching placed special emphasis on memorization in addition to reading, writing and arithmetic. The student-teacher relationship was not informal but pure and sincere. The educands respected their educators and had absolute faith in them. The parents had total confidence in the educators and willingly entrusted their wards to the care of the teachers. The teachers had a paternal attitude towards their wards. This was particularly important since most of the educational institutions were residential. The salary of the teachers was not very high but the lacuna was amply filled up by gifts and respect. There was a system of reward and punishment to maintain order and discipline in educational institutions. Scholars had a place of respect in society as they used to have in ancient Indian period.

The above brief description shows that medieval Indian philosophy of education was built up by Hindus and Muslims together. As Sarojini Naidu has aptly remarked, "The impact of the Muslims and the Hindus has evolved the present Indian culture. We cannot, even if we are foolish enough to try, untwist this closely inter-twisted and inter-twined unity of culture that makes modern India."[39]

Modern Indian Philosophy of Education

Modern Indian philosophy of education started under the British rule. After firmly establishing themselves as rulers of India the British recruited educated Indians to carry on administrative and official work. As the Indians educated in Hindu or Muslim institutions were not useful for working of the British Government, therefore, Lord Macaulay drew up a plan of western oriented education in India. On February 8, 1935 Macaulay presented his historical '*minits*' making a bitter attack upon Indian literature and culture. He laid stress on what he called religious objectivity which meant the duty of England to teach Indians what was good for their health. The policy developed on the basis of Macaulay's educational views gave primacy to the propagation of European literature and science, suspension of scholarships for students, neglect of publication of Eastern literature and encouragement to propagation of English literature. This policy was accepted by Lord Bentinck.

When Lord Auckland succeeded Lord Macaulay as India's Governor General, some critics of Macaulay's policy presented a memorandum to him. Lord Auckland increased the educational grant for the orientalists, gave primacy to oriental studies, increased the number of scholarships and made arrangements for printing and publication of oriental works. However, East India Company only employed those who have received English education. Therefore, the demand for English education increased. A significant change in the field of education was its intimate link with livelihood. Domestic crafts were neglected and many artisans and craftsmen sought employment in British factories. Professional and vocational institutions started to provide education in medicine, engineering law and other specialised areas. In 1853 the British Parliament reviewed company's charter and the Select Committee declared that English education in India was useful. Charles Wood published his declaration regarding education on 19th July, 1853. This declaration considered providing education as the foremost duty of the Government. However, the aim of education did not change. Its purpose was mainly creation of cogs for the British machinery in India. However, along with the study of western language and literature, the study of oriental literature was also given a place in the curriculum. Both English and Indian languages were accepted as the medium of instruction. It is clear that Wood's Dispatch cannot be referred as the *Magna Carta* of Indian Education.

Education during 1857—1947

After war of independence in 1857 the reins of India's administration passed into the hands of British Parliament. Wood's Dispatch had already finished the monopoly of Christian missionaries over education in India. General Council of Education of India in England asked Lord Rippon, the Viceroy, to carry out a survey of education in India. Rippon appointed what was known as Hunter Commission to survey education in India. The Commission surveyed primary, secondary, higher, religious and women education in India, and made important recommendations, of which the most important were as follows:

1. Provision in education must be made for Muslims, *Harijans*, tribals, hill people and members of royal families.
2. Indian institutions should be provided aid.

3. Scholarships must be provided to local institutions.
4. The responsibility for higher education should be entrusted to local people with Government aid.
5. The Education Department should run institutions of higher learning in the country.
6. Students should be given complete freedom of religious education.

Besides Hunter Commission, another landmark in modern Indian history of education was Indian University's Commission, 1902. The Commission made the following important recommendations:

1. New universities should not be established.
2. The constitutions of universities should be changed to make provisions for teaching in the universities.
3. Under-graduate and post-graduate colleges should be introduced.
4. Conditions for recognising colleges should be stern.
5. The syndicates should have from 9 to 15 members.
6. The standard of the metric examination should be improved.

The Indian Universities Act, 1904 was formulated on the basis of these recommendations. Lord Curzon made significant efforts for the progress of higher education in India. However, the demand for a nationalist policy of education in India was raised at the Calcutta Session of Indian National Congress in 1906. The demand asked for Indian control of the educational system. It denounced imitation of the West though appreciated Western knowledge and science. It asked for more vocational education. Though the Government did not give much hearing to this demand, it inspired a nationalist wave for education throughout the country. This led to the emergence of such institutions as Santiniketan, Gurukul Kangri, Jamia Milia Islamia, Gujarat Vidyapith, Kashi Vidyapith, the Women's University (SNDT), etc. These institutions had a distinctly national character. In 1912, the Government announced its educational policy with the proposal of making primary education village-oriented. It provided replacement of Government aided institutions by institutions managed by local bodies. The school education was separated from higher education. After the First World War, the

Government appointed Calcutta University Commission also known as Sadler Commission. The report of Sadler Commission was formulated on the basis of Halden's report on London University. It laid down the structures of Mysore, Patna, Banaras, Aligarh, Dacca, Lucknow, Hyderabad besides Calcutta University.

In 1929, Hertog Committee reviewed education in India. It pointed out stagnation and extravagance in primary education. It analysed the problem of failing candidates in secondary education. It made recommendation for the betterment of female education in India. In 1934 Sapru Committee reviewed the problem of unemployment in U.P. and suggested introducing vocational subjects at the secondary level. In 1936-37 Abbot-Wood presented their recommendations for polytechnic institutions in the country. On October 2, 1937 M.K. Gandhi presented his 7-year scheme of basic primary education. It was formulated by Wardha Committee under the chairmanship of Dr. Zakir Hussain. On the recommendation of the committee basic education was organised by Hindustani Talimi Sangh.

Sergeant Commission, 1944 recommended for distinction between academic and technical institutions though both should aim at integral education.

The British control over education ended with the freedom of India on 15th August, 1947 and with it ended the period of modern Indian education as distinguished from contemporary period. The British Educational System initiated Western influence of education in India. It created social and political awareness in the country. It introduced modern western science which resulted in the rise of famous Indian scientists including J.C. Bose, Ramanujam, C.V. Raman. It inspired literary and cultural consciousness and developed nationalistic feelings. However, it was definitely British-oriented. Its avowed aim was to serve British interest. It was colonial in aim and practice. The medium of instruction was a hindrance in the development of creativity. Sometimes it encouraged communal passions. The Christian missionaries and the British administrators encouraged Christian teachings in educational institutions. Thus, the British philosophy of education in modern period did not change appreciably from its beginning in Macaulay's thought. In spite of all the enquiries of the Commissions and their recommendations, this educational philosophy was not conducive to national welfare.

Contemporary Indian Philosophy of Education

Due to the above mentioned defects of the British philosophy of education as practised in India in modern period, Indian thinkers and educationists have bitterly criticised it. One finds criticism of this philosophy of education by almost all the contemporary Indian philosophers of education including Swami Vivekananda, Sri Aurobindo, Swami Dayananda, M.K. Gandhi, Rabindra Nath Tagore, Sarvapalli Radhakrishnan, J.L. Nehru and M.N. Roy. Both the traditionalists and the Western oriented thinkers were equally critical of the British philosophy of education in India. They could clearly see that its aims and means were against national interest. Therefore, long before India achieved freedom, these illustrious thinkers particularly Vivekananda, Sri Aurobindo and Rabindra Nath Tagore criticised the prevalent philosophy of education and presented alternative philosophies. The reformists including Raja Ram Mohan Roy, Mr. Annie Besant, M.G. Ranade and others asked for reforms in education. The philosophers of education suggested plans for national education.

The Traditional and West Oriented Thinkers

Though nationalists in orientation and reformists in purpose, contemporary Indian philosophers of education differed in their sources of inspiration. While Vivekananda, Sri Aurobindo, Dayananda, M.K. Gandhi, Rabindra Nath and Sarvapalli Radhakrishnan drew inspiration from ancient Indian philosophy of education, J.L. Nehru and M.N. Roy were inspired by the Western philosophy of education. Thus, Vivekananda, Sri Aurobindo, Dayananda, M.K. Gandhi, Rabindra Nath and Sarvapalli Radhakrishnan may be said to belong to the traditional group of contemporary Indian philosophers of education. This traditional group could be identified by the following characteristics:

1. *Neo-Vedanta philosophical basis*: Traditionalist Indian philosophy of education, like ancient Indian philosophy of

education, drew inspiration from *Vedanta* philosophy. It only reinterpreted the ancient *Vedanta* philosophy in the light of new knowledge. Therefore, it has been rightly called *Neo-Vedanta* philosophy. It is new since it synthesises religion and science, ancient Indian wisdom and modern Western thought. It considered the *Vedas*, the *Upanisads* and the *Bhagavadgita* as the representatives of Indian wisdom. It accepted the educational philosophy presented in these scriptures, suggesting modifications according to contemporary conditions. Thus, it is not revivalist but reformist in approach. It shows a return to self- analysis and self-evaluation by India's foremost thinkers. This was the result of the contrast which they witnessed in the conditions of their own countrymen *vis-a-vis* the men and women of western countries. They compared the ancient Indian educational philosophy with the ideas of modern western thinkers and found that they were no less valuable in contemporary Indian situations then they in ancient time. These thinkers were inspired by nationalism and the ideal of *Swadesi* and *Svadharma* on the one hand and world brotherhood and internationalism on the other. Therefore, their thinking was nowhere conservative, narrow or reactionary. They presented a philosophy of education founded upon man's status in the cosmos and the human nature. All of them visualised a religion of humanity to form the basis of national scheme of education.

2. ***Integral approach***: Besides *Vedanta* philosophy, another characteristic of the philosophical foundations of the traditional type of contemporary Indian philosophy of education is an integral approach. This integral approach may be found in almost every field of education, the aims, the means, the curriculum, the educator-educand relationship, teaching methods, school administration, etc. Integral approach is against one-sided solutions. It insists upon including every element within the whole, serving welfare of every constituent of the group. Everywhere ancient prescriptions have been supported though they were balanced according to contemporary conditions.

3. ***Integral psychology***: Ancient Indian approach to human psychology was integral. Man has been always defined by Indian thinkers as a finite-infinite being. Human nature has been always explained in terms of the higher and not in terms of the lower

urges as it has been in West. Indian psychology has been idealistic in nature. It has close links with religion and metaphysics. All these characteristics may be found in the interpretation of human nature advanced by traditional contemporary Indian philosophers of education. They, however, never neglected the needs of the physical world. Swami Vivekananda and Sri Aurobindo particularly emphasised the need of physical development in the achievement of educational ideal. All these thinkers equally laid emphasis upon all types of education.

4. *Synthesis of idealism and pragmatism*: *Though* contemporary Indian philosophy of education is rooted in *Vedanta* idealism, these philosophers presented very pragmatic and practical scheme of education. They suggested diversification of curriculum, education of senses, education of the mind, vocational education, education for livelihood and education for elimination of poverty. Each of them was conscious of the appalling poverty of the country and, therefore, they understood the importance of pragmatic value of education. All of them insisted upon using the mother tongue as the medium of primary education. All of them accepted the need of developing Hindi as the *lingua franca*. All of them, however, agreed to retain English as an important part of higher education. All of them advocated nationalist system of education.

The above characteristics of the philosophy of education of the traditional school do not prove that philosophies of education presented by these thinkers were identical in details. All of them have presented original ideas in different fields of education. The above characteristics only show areas of agreement in philosophical foundation and basic postulates. This will be more clear as we examine the philosophies of education of these thinkers in subsequent chapters. The final picture will he clear only in the conclusion.

Besides the group of contemporary Indian philosophers of education drawing inspiration from ancient Indian philosophy, another group of contemporary Indian philosophers of education drew inspiration from Western philosophy of education. This group is particularly represented by J.L. Nehru and M.N. Roy. These two thinkers almost nowhere borrowed their philosophical ideas from ancient Indian scriptures. Well versed in Western thought as they were, they founded their educational theories on naturalistic humanism. Radical humanism of M.N. Roy was a brand of Western naturalistic humanism. Different from the religious humanism of the traditionalist contemporary Indian philosophers of education, the educational ideas of these thinkers form a part of their general, social and political theory. They had firsthand knowledge of contemporary Indian politics and presented philosophies of education in the context of their general schemes of social and political reformation. The characteristics of these thinkers will be further clear as we examine them in details in subsequent chapters. Both these class of thinkers will be compared in the concluding part of the thesis.

References

1. *Manusmriti* (M.S.), II, 146.
2. *Ibid.,* 145.
3. *Gautama*, II, 56.
4. *Yajnavalkya Smriti* (Y.S.), I, 35.
5. *Gautama,* I, 10, 11; *Vasistha Dharma Sutra* (V. D. S.), III, 21; M.S. II, 140.
6. *Nirukta*, I, 4.
7. *Apastamba Dharma Sutra* (A. D. S.), I, 1.1.14.
8. *M.S.*, II, 69.
9. *Ibid.*, II, 141.
10. Y.S., I, 34.
11. *Visnu Dharma Sutra* (Vis. D.S.), 32-1-2.
12. *M.S.*, II, 149.
13. *A.D.S.*, I,1.1.11.
14. *Ibid.*, I. 1-1-12-13.
15. *Vayu Purana (*V.P.) Vol. I, 59-29.
16. M.S., II, 70-74.
17. *Ibid.*, II, 165.
18. *Y.S.*, I, 40.
19. Dutt, N.K., *Origin and Growth of Caste in India,* (Calcutta: The Book Co., 1931), p. 182.
20. Crawford, S. Cromwell, *Evolution of Hindu Ethical Ideals*, p. 96.
21. Dutt, N.K., *op. cit.*, p. 182.

22. *Chhandogya,* IV, 4.5; 3.5; VII, 15.1.
23. *M.S.,* II, 198, 180-381.
24. *A.D.S.,* I, 1.3.11-23; I, 1.2.28-30; I, 2.5.26.
25. *Baudhayana Dharma Sutra* (B.D.S.), 37; *Gautama,* 1,1.2.34.
26. *M.S.,* H, 194-198; *A.D.S.,* I, 2.5, 26; *Gautama,* II, 20-21.
27. *Ibid.,* 200-201.
28. *Ibid.*
29. *Ibid.*
30. *A.D.S.,* I, 2.8.15.
31. *M.S.,* II, 128.
32. *A.D.S.,* I, 2.5,19; I, 3.10.17.
33. *A.D.S.,* I, 2.8.25-28.
34. *M.S.,* II, 92.
35. *Ibid.,* II, 118.
36. Kane, P.V., *History of Dharmasastras* (Pune: Bhandarkar Oriental Research Institute, 1941), Vol. II, Part I, p. 369.
37. *Ibid.,* p. 370.
38. *Ibid.*
39. Dr. Sorojini Naidu—'The Bombay Chronicle'—quoted from K.S. Vakil and S. Natrajan's *Education in India,* 1966, p. 42.

3

Swami Vivekananda's Philosophy of Education

In the neo-Vedanta humanistic tradition of contemporary Indian thought Vivekananda presented a philosophy of education for man making. Amongst the contemporary Indian philosophers of education he is one of those who revolted against the imposition of British system of education in India. He was severely critical of the pattern of education introduced by the British in India. He felt that the current system of education did not confirm to India's culture. He pointed out that such an education only brings about an external change without any profound inner force.

Criticism of Contemporary Educational System

Against the contemporary educational system the chief objection raised by Vivekananda was that it turned men into slaves, capable of slavery and nothing else. About the prevailing university education, he remarked that it was no better than an efficient machine for rapidly turning out clerks. It deprived people of their faith and belief. The English educated people believed that *Gita* was false and the *Vedas* were no more significant than rural folk lore. Criticising this system of education Vivekananda compared it to the person who wanted to turn his ass into a horse, was advised to thrash the ass in order to achieve this transformation and killed his ass in this process. Vivekananda also criticised the contemporary system of education from the humanistic viewpoint. He was a humanist and pleaded for education for man-making. Such was not the education propounded by the British. Therefore, Vivekananda condemned it. He remarked, "It is not a man-making education, it is merely and entirely a negative education. A negative education or any training that is based on negation, is worse than death. The child is taken to school, and the first thing he learns is that his father is a fool, the second thing that his grandfather is lunatic, the third thing that all his teachers are hypocrites, the fourth, that all the sacred books are lies. By the time he is sixteen he is a mass of negation, lifeless and boneless. And the result is that fifty years of such education has not produced one original man in the three presidencies. Every man of originality that has been produced has been educated elsewhere, and not in this country, or they have gone to the old universities once more to cleanse themselves of superstitions."[1]

Aims of Education

Education for Self-development

In contrast to the contemporary system of education Vivekananda advocated education for self-development. He said, "By education I do not mean the present system, but something in the line of positive teaching. Mere book learning won't do. We want that education by which character is formed, strength of mind is increased, the intellect is expanded and by which one can stand on one's own feet. What we want are Western science coupled with *Vedanta*, '*Brahmacarya*' as guiding motto, and also *sradha* and faith in one's own self."[2] These words by Vivekananda represent the characteristic Indian definition of education. Education according to most of the Western educationists aim at man's adjustment with the environment. According to the Indian philosophical tradition, on the other hand, education is the realisation of the knowledge inherent in man. True knowledge does not come from outside, it is discovered with the individual, in the self which is the source of all knowledge. To quote Vivekananda again, "All knowledge that the world has ever received comes from the mind; the infinite library of the universe is in your own mind. The external world is simply the suggestion, the occasion, which sets you to study your own mind, but the object of your study is always your own mind. The falling of an apple gave the suggestion to Newton, and he studied his own mind. He rearranged all the precious links of thought in his mind and discovered a new link among them, which we call the law of gravitation."[3] Thus according to Vivekananda, the function of education is the uncovering of the knowledge hidden in our own mind. Education is the process of self-development. In the words of Vivekananda, "You cannot teach a child any more than you can grow a plant. The plant develops its own nature."[4] A person's education is not judged by the number of books he has read but by the thickness of the cover of ignorance on his mind. The thicker is this cover, the greater is the ignorance. As the light of knowledge dawns this cover of ignorance gradually shatters. The teacher's job is to uncover knowledge by his guidance. His guidance makes the mind active and the educand himself unveils the knowledge lying within him.

Fulfillment of Svadharma

Vivekananda supported the idea of *Svadharma* in education. Everyone has to grow like himself. No one has to copy others. It is hence that he condemned the imposition of foreign education. He asked, "Getting by heart the thoughts of others in a foreign language and stuffing your brain with them and taking some university degree, you can pride yourself as educated. Is this education?"[5] True improvement is self-inspired. There should be no external pressure of any type on the child. External pressure only creates destructive reactions leading to obstinacy and indiscipline. In an atmosphere of freedom, love and sympathy alone, the child will develop courage and self-reliance. He should not be unnecessarily checked in his activities. The educator should not constantly tell him to do this or that. Such negative directions tend to blunt his intelligence and mental development. He should be talked to stand on his own, to be himself. This is so since as Vivekananda suggests, "If you do not allow once to become a lion, he will become a fox."[6] Therefore, education should be modified to suit the individual child. Each child should be given opportunities to develop according to his own inner nature.

Thus, Vivekananda is against any type of external pressure upon the child. He is a staunch champion of freedom in education. Freedom is the first requirement for self-development. The child should be given freedom to grow, according to his own nature. In the words of Vivekananda, "You cannot teach a child anymore than you can grow a plant. All you can do is on the negative side—you can only help. You can take away the obstacles, but knowledge comes out of its own nature. Loosen the soil a little, so that it may come out easily. Put a hedge around it, see that it is not killed by anything, and there your work stops. You cannot do anything else. The rest is a manifestation from within its own nature."[7] The teacher should not exert any type of pressure on the child. The child should be helped in solving his problems himself. The teachers should have an attitude of service and workshop. Education ultimately aims at realisation. It is meant to the establishment of a fraternity of mankind.

Education for Character

Character is the solid foundation for self-development. The aim of education as self-development, therefore, leads to the aim of education for character. Defining character, Vivekananda said, "The character of any man is but the aggregate of his tendencies, the sum total of the bent of his mind. As pleasure and pain pass before his soul, they leave upon it different pictures and the result of these combined impressions is what is called a man's character."[8] The aim of education is character building. This depends upon the ideals cherished by the individual. The educator should present high ideals before the educands. The best way to develop a character is the personal example of high character set by the teachers. Laying emphasis upon this point Vivekananda said, "Without the personal life of the teacher there would be no education. One would live from his very boyhood with one whose character is like a blazing fire, and should have before him a living example of the highest teaching. . . . The charge of imparting knowledge should again fall upon the shoulders of '*tyagis*'."[9] In ancient Indian system of education the teachers used to present high ideals before the pupils, who in their turn imitated those ideals according to their capacities.

Character formation, according to Vivekananda, requires hard work. This is not possible by those who have a wish for all types of enjoyments. Struggle is the best teacher in character building. Activity and *purushartha* are the signs of life. Inactivity shows absence of vitality. While living in all types of comforts and escaping from all types of labour, no one can build up high character.

Besides hard work, character formation requires traits such' as purity, thirst for knowledge, preservance, faith, humility, submission and veneration, etc. These qualities may be developed by the teacher's example and the pupil's efforts. According to Vivekananda, "Without faith, humility, submission and veneration in our hearts towards the teacher, there cannot be any growth in us. In those countries which have neglected to keep up this kind of relation, the teacher has become a mere lecturer, the teacher expecting his five dollar and the person taught expecting his brain to be filled with the teacher's words and each going his own way after this much is done. The true teacher is he who can immediately come down to the level of the student, and transfer his soul to the student's soul and see through and understand through his mind."[10]

Such a relationship between the teacher and the taught is possible only in a *Gurukul* system of education. Therefore, Vivekananda favoured the ancient Indian *Gurukul* system of education. In these *Gurukuls* the pupils served the teacher, in his turn helped the pupils everywhere to achieve knowledge. There was hardly any economic relationship between the teacher and taught, which is the curse of the present system of education.

Character is intimately connected with habits. Habits express character. Good habits make for good character. While the contemporary psychologists admit the value of habits in one's life, Vivekananda has pointed out the value of habits not only in this life but in lives to come. A bad habit may be broken by developing the opposite good habits. If a man constantly thinks that he will be courageous and progressive, he may develop confidence for breaking bad habits. It is not the teacher or the guardian who may reform the habits of a person but only he himself. Man is caught in the net of his own *karmas* from which he alone can get out, no one else can directly help him. Our own self in us our best guide in the struggle that is life. The child should be allowed to commit mistakes in the process of character formation. He will learn much by his mistakes. Errors are the stepping stones to our progress in character. This progress requires courage and strong will. Strong will is the sign of great character. Will makes men great. Therefore, there is no occasion to be discouraged or to weep, one should exercise his will and he will see that things which he considered to be impossible become easy and possible. Vivekananda himself was an ideal teacher. His words worked like magic upon men and women. This is possible only in the case of a teacher who has himself risen high. Presenting his own example, Vivekananda asked the people to build up their character and manifest their real nature which is the Effulgent, the Resplendent, the Ever Pure.

Means of Education

The best means of education, according to Vivekananda is love. Education should be based upon love. Love is the best inspiration in character building. The child should be taught through love. This love for men, for human beings. The only motive in imparting education should be love for the educand, for the man in him. That is why Vivekananda's philosophy of education is known as education for man-making. The teacher's aim should be neither money making nor attainment of fame but only bestowing human love. The spiritual force works through love. This love within the educator is the real source of his influence upon the educand. This may be amply clear by the example of the relationship of Vivekananda with his Guru Ramakrishna. It was the force of spiritual love in Ramakrishna which helped Vivekananda to God realisation. It is this which makes the educator to take the educand from untruth to truth, darkness to light, death to immortality. The task of the educator is to help the educand in manifesting and expressing his abilities and capacities. Education should help the individual to recognise his cultural heritage and to use it in his struggle of life. The educator can guide the educand because he himself has the experience of treading on this path and knows how to face its difficulties. Vivekananda has not only presented high ideals of education but also developed a sound system by which these ideals may be achieved.

Education is not a bed of roses. Every educand has to face problems peculiarly his own. He solves them by his own efforts and with the guidance of the teacher. The skilled teacher guides the pupil through these difficulties and takes him forward. This requires a sufficient knowledge of human psychology because most of our problems are psychological in nature. The teacher should teach the educand to concentrate his attention, only then can the problems be solved. The greater the attention, the more is the effort effective.

Concentration, according to ancient Indian thought, is the key to true knowledge. Therefore, Vivekananda has placed much emphasis upon focusing of attention. It is only after years of concentration that a man becomes a scholar and a great scientist. The educands should be distinguished according to their abilities, everyone of them has to develop concentration. Again, while teaching concentration the educator should keep in mind the varying abilities of concentration possessed by the educands. While for some persons concentration is spontaneous and easy, for others it is difficult and requires long training. Hence the educator must organise his teaching in such a way that he may be helpful to each educand separately. He should attend to every one's difficulties and try to solve them as much as possible. Thus Vivekananda supported the ancient Indian means of achieving concentration.

Again, according to ancient Indian thinkers, *Brahmacarya* or abstinence is the first means of achieving concentration. It gives mental and spiritual powers of the highest kind. It transforms sex drive into a spiritual force. *Brahmacarya* implies purity of thought, deed and action. It helps to improve and sharpen various psychological processes such as learning, remembering, thinking, etc. It helps in achieving power of memory and improve the powers of the mind. Vivekananda, therefore, strongly emphasised the need for the students to observe *Brahmacarya*. This leads to both mental and physical advantages. Firstly, it takes effective care of all distractions. Secondly, it improves the body and the mind so that they may become effective means of knowledge.

In addition to concentration the other means of education are discussion and contemplation. It is only through these that the educand may remove his difficulties. Discussion should be carried out in an informal atmosphere. Contemplation should be practiced in a calm and quiet atmosphere with the mind fully alive. In the end the educational process requires faith and reverence of the educand in the teacher and his teachings. Without faith and reverence no true knowledge can be achieved. It is faith and reverence which are the sound foundations for all character development and self-education. This faith and reverence, however, depend not only upon the educand but also upon the high examples presented by the teacher. In the educational process, therefore, the teacher also occupies a very high place.

Types of Education

Science and Vedanta

With the aim of education as man-making, Vivekananda developed a curriculum which could lead to multisided and all round development of the educand. He tried to synthesise science and *Vedanta*, modern and ancient knowledge so that the curriculum may involve whatever is best in these. He realised that the curriculum must be able to achieve the development of every aspect of the child's personality. With this aim in view he laid emphasis upon the scientific education on the one side and the teaching of *Vedanta* on the other. According to him what is really needed in India is a harmony between Western Science and Indian *Vedanta*. If this is not done it may lead to improper use of science in the form of invention of destructive weapons.

Training in Art

Besides the provision of science and *Vedanta*, Vivekananda considered art as an indispensable part of the curriculum. Education in science must be supplemented by training in art. According to Vivekananda while Asians specialised in Art, the West developed science and both are necessary for modern man. The ideal of utility should be substituted by the ideal of duty through the teaching of art.

Medium of Education

In the teaching of languages Vivekananda laid particular stress upon teaching through the mother tongue. Here he is supported by all other contemporary Indian philosophers of education. Besides mother tongue, there should be a common language which is necessary to keep the country united. This may be taught in addition to the regional languages. The teaching of Sanskrit forms an important part of the curriculum envisaged by Vivekananda. Sanskrit is the source of all Indian languages and a repository of all inherited knowledge. It is, therefore, absolutely necessary that every Indian should know Sanskrit. Vivekananda appreciated the greatness of Sanskrit in eloquent words when he said that this language granted power, ability and prestige to the nation and that our awareness of our cultural heritage and past greatness depends very much upon our knowledge of this language. He felt that in the absence of this knowledge, it will be impossible to protect Indian culture. If the society has to develop and progress it is necessary that men and women should know the language which is the store house of ancient heritage, besides the knowledge of the mother tongue.

Teaching Methods

Vivekananda elaborately discussed the teaching methods in physical, moral and religious education. This, discussion gives an idea of types of education as well as methods of teaching.

Physical Education

Vivekananda laid particular stress on the value of physical education in curriculum. He said, "You will be nearer to Heaven through-football than through the study of *Gita.* You will understand *Gita* better by your biceps, your muscles a little stronger . . . you will understand the *Upanisads* better and the glory of the *Atman*, when your body stands firm on your feet and you feel yourself as man."[11] Self-realisation or character building is impossible in the absence of physical education. One must know the secret of making the body strong through physical education for a complete education it is necessary to develop both mind and the body. Vivekananda himself took physical exercise every day. He glorified power and opposed weakness in any form. Power is life and weakness is death. Not only this, but in his opinion, power was happiness and weakness a never ending burden. It is hence that he so much emphasised the importance of physical education particularly for young men and women.

Moral and Religious Education

Laying emphasis upon religious education Vivekananda said, "Religion is the inner most core of education. I do not mean my own or anyone else's opinion about religion. Religion is as the rice and everything else, like the curries. Taking only curries causes indigestion, and so is the case with taking rice alone."[12] Therefore, religious education is a vital part of a sound curriculum. This religious education is necessary in order to counter effect the evil influences of modern materialism. It is only by a synthesis of religion and science that man may reap the advantage of both. As has been already pointed out, religious education in itself is never sufficient. It should not be the whole of curriculum but only a part of it. This religion, again, is not any particular dogma or sectarian philosophy, in fact it is what Tagore called religion of man. It is hence that Vivekananda did not distinguished between secular and religious education. He thought that the former may be given by the latter. He said, "We have to give them secular education. We have to follow the plan laid down by our ancestors, that is, to bring all the ideals slowly down among the masses. Raise them slowly up, raise them to equality. Impart ... secular knowledge through religion."[13]

The best way of imparting religious education is to present the high ideals of saints and religious men before the students. They should be taught to worship saints to follow their ideals. Among the great souls, Vivekananda pointed out are *Rama*, *Krisna*, *Mahavir* and *Ramakrisna*. In the ideal of *Sri Krisna* he laid more emphasis on his personality as the author of *Gita*. He said, "Keep aside for the present the *Vrindavan* aspect of *Sri Krisna,* and spread far and wide the worship of *Sri Krisna* roaring out the *Gita* with the voice of a lion; and bring into daily use the worship of *Sakti*—the *Divine Mother*, the source of all power. We now mostly need the ideal of the hero with the tremendous spirit of *rajas* thrilling through his veins from head to foot, the hero who will dare and die to know the truth, the hero whose armour is renunciation, whose sword is wisdom; we want the spirit of the brave warrior in the battle field."[14] Thus,

Vivekananda wanted men and women to develop qualities according to their particular sex and their role in society. He asked young men to develop manly qualities. Even in religious practice he considered courage to be a higher quality. Religion is not mere ritualism. It is a progress towards high ideals in the face of extreme difficulties.

Besides courage, Vivekananda prescribed service and devotion in religious education. For this purpose he eulogised the ideal of *Hamtman* who was a living example of service, devotion and courage. He deplored the dramatic imitation of *Ras Lila* because it is against the interest of the country at present. Purity is the real basis of the country at present. Even in music Vivekananda advised young men to adopt manly music so that it may infuse bravery and courage. This, however, does not mean that Vivekananda rejected any particular type of religious practice. He only wanted to adapt religious practices according to the needs of the time. India, according to him, today needs a religion which should be harmonious with science and teach patriotism, service and sacrifice. Then alone religious education may be useful to the nation. Religion influences total man. It encourages all type of qualities, soft as well as virile. Vivekananda emphasised the inculcation of the latter type of virtues. He exhorted young men by saying, "Never allow weakness to overtake: your mind. Remember Mahavir, remember the *Divine Mother*, and you will see that all weakness, all cowardice will vanish at once."[15]

It goes without saying that such a moral and religious education will develop self-confidence among young men and women. Self-confidence, according to Vivekananda, is the real religion. It includes world brotherhood and love of humanity, because a person having self-confidence sees his self-everywhere. In fact, self-confidence means confidence in humanity. Thus Vivekananda's religion was humanistic. Religion is the source of all powers. It is again, the source of all goods. Thus, for Vivekananda, ethics and religion are one and the same. God is always on the side of goodness. To fight for goodness is, therefore, service to God. Weakness is the source of all evils. It is at the root of all violence, hatred and enmity. If a man sees his own self everywhere he need not fear anyone. Fearlessness and power are eternal truths, the real nature of the self. Thus Vivekananda pleaded for realisation of truth through religious practices. Long before Gandhi identified truth with God, Vivekananda called truth God. The seeker after truth should search for it in every aspect of life. Truth is power, untruth is weakness. Knowledge is truth, ignorance is untruth. Thus truth increases power, courage and energy. It is light giving. It is, therefore, necessary for the individual as well as collective welfare.

Thus Vivekananda worshipped power. This power, however, was not physical or biological as that of Nietzsche. It was spiritual power. Rising high in the tradition of *Vedanta* Vivekananda never allowed his feet to leave the solid ground. His teachings influenced the West where materialism was rampant. This was due to the reason that his teachings were based upon universal truths. Modern man is not prepared to leave the world. He wants to enjoy it. Vivekananda, therefore, gave a practical garb to his religion. India in his time was groaning under slavery. Vivekananda, therefore, asked Indian men and women to shed all types of weakness and to march forward courageously. According to him we have to speak less and work more, achieve power first than anything else. To quote Vivekananda, "First of all our young men must be strong. Religion will come afterwards."[16]

In the curriculum for religious education Vivekananda considered *Gita*, *Upanisads* and the *Vedas* as the most important. The study of these scriptures will fill young men and women with courage. India has lived by their force, and will continue to be living by their inspiration. These are the eternal sources of the life force of Indian culture. These are the bases of our spiritual education. Vivekananda, however, was not in favour of preaching any particular religious dogmas. Religion for him was self-realisation. Temples, mosques, churches and synagogues do not make religion. Religion is divinization. It is not intellectual development but transformation of total man. It is nothing if it does not teach us service and sacrifice. It is the basis for character formation. It should lead to man-making. In tune with his Guru Rama-krishna, Vivekananda pleaded for unity of world religions. He considered all religions to be equal. A true religion cannot be limited to a particular place or time. The religious books, teachers and institutions are eternal. Their ancient forms are worshipped and their modern forms are respected. Thus, in his moral and religious education Vivekananda pleaded for the education of unity of world religions.

Education for Different Sections of Society

Vivekananda respected human individuality everywhere and pleaded for freedom for everyone. Each soul, according to him, "is potentially divine. The goal is to manifest this Divinity within by controlling nature, external and internal. Do this, either by work, or worship, or psychic centre or philosophy—by one or more or all of these—and be free. This is the whole of religion. Doctrines or dogmas, or rituals or books, temples or forms are secondary details."[17] It was due to his devotion for the poor and backward people that Vivekananda wanted to make education an instrument for the upliftment of the masses. Like Gandhi after him, Vivekananda throughout his life, worked for the uplift of backward classes. He pleaded for universal education so that these backward people may fall in line with others. He said, "A nation is advanced in proportion as education and intelligence is spread among the masses. The chief causes of India's ruin have been the monopolizing of the whole education and intelligence of the land among the handful of men. If we are to rise again, we shall have to do it by spreading education among masses."[18] Thus, education should spread to every household in the country, to factories, playing grounds and agricultural fields. If the children do not come to the school, the teacher should reach them. Two or three educated men should team up, collect all the paraphernalia of education and should go to the village to impart education to the children. Thus, Vivekananda favoured education for different sections of society, rich and poor, young and old, male and female.

In the education of women Vivekananda laid particular stress on chastity and fearlessness. He conceived an ideal institution for women known as *Math* where literature and religion may be taught. Pointing out to the curriculum in this institution he said, "Other matters such as sewing, culinary art, rules of domestic work, and upbringing of children will also be taught while '*Japa*' worship and meditation, etc., shall form an indispensable part of the teaching. The duty of the teaching in school ought to devolve in every respect on educated widows and '*Brahmacarinis*' It is good to avoid in this country any association of men with women's schools."[19] Thus, he presented a comprehensive, curriculum for women so that they may develop high character, courage and confidence. He presented the ideal of Sita and lamented that modern Indian women are imitating western ideals which had led to all round degeneration. Like males he advised females also to observe *Brahmacarya* which is a solid foundation for any type of education. He was extremely sorry for the lowly condition of Indian women. He considered women to be the incarnation of power and asked men to respect them in every way. He pointed out that unless Indian women secure a respectable place in this country, the nation can never march forward. The regeneration of Indian women, according to him, depends upon proper education. Women's education should be in the hands of women. Clarifying his scheme in this connection he said, "After five or six years' training in this '*Math*', the guardians of the girls may marry them. If deemed fit for '*Yoga*' and religious life, with the permission of their guardians they will be allowed to stay in this *Math*, taking the vow of celibacy. These celibate nuns will in time be the teachers and preachers of the *Math*. In villages and towns they will open centres and strive for the spread of female education. Through such devout preachers of character there will be the real spread of female education in this country . . . Spirituality, sacrifice and self-control will be the motto of the pupils of this *Math,* and service or '*Seva Dharma*' the vow of their life . . . If the life of the women of this country be moulded in such fashion, then only will there be the re-appearance of such ideal characters of *Sita, Savitri* and *Gargi*"[20]

Critical Evaluation

Our discussion about Vivekananda's concept of the aims and ideals of education, its process and curriculum has made it amply clear that he was a humanist in the true sense of the term. He said, "Look upon every man, woman and everyone as God. Blessed you are that privilege was given to you when other had it not. Do it only as a worship. The only God to worship is the human soul in the human body. Of course, all animals are temples too, but man is the highest, the *Taj Mahal* of temples. If I cannot worship in that, no other temple will, be of any advantage."[21] Vivekananda's humanism, however, was different from naturalistic humanism. It is in this background that his education for man-making should be understood. Man, according to him, is the highest of all living beings so much so that according to Vivekananda even the angels will have to come down again and again for salvation through a human body.

The educational ideals advocated by Vivekananda have been supported by most of the modern Western educationists. Education today is defined as the process of all round development of the child. Such a development can take place only from within, while the external environment provides occasion for such development. The teacher has to provide the environment so that the child may become aware of the treasure of knowledge lying buried in his mind. Modern psychologists point out that in every individual there are certain dormant powers which have to be developed through education. The teacher's real job is to see that there should be no impediments in the child's path to self-development. He is like a gardener who prepares grounds for the growth of his plants, protects them and nourishes them so that the plant may grow properly. Similarly, the teacher takes care of the child, provides him a suitable environment and looks after his proper growth. Thus though education comes from within, the teacher is an indispensable part of it. While the motivation comes from within, the teacher activates it. He encourages the child to use his mind, body and sense organs. Thus Vivekananda presented a positive system of education. He wrote, "Education is the manifestation of the perfection already in man. I look upon religion as the innermost core of education."[22] In his philosophy of education Vivekananda synthesized spiritual and material values. He felt that India needed a system of education based on the ancient *Vedanta* but at the same time worthy of making individual earn his livelihood so that the country may progress. He maintained that no profession is bad provided it is done with a sense of service and self-sacrifice. It is the absence of this dignity of labour which is responsible for the degraded condition of this country. Long before M.K. Gandhi, Vivekananda pleaded for the worship of God in poor. He said, "So long as the millions live in hunger and ignorance, I hold every man a traitor who having been educated at their expense pays not the least heed to them."[23] He asked young men to change the situation. He pleaded for universal, compulsory and free education. He asked the educator to reach every village and every hutment so that the whole country may awake from ignorance.

References

1. *Swami Vivekananda on India and Her Problems*, p. 48
2. *Ibid.*, p. 51.
3. Vivekananda, S., *C.W.* (1984), Vol. I, p. 28.
4. *Ibid.*, Vol. V, p. 324.
5. *Ibid.*, Vol. VII, p. 146.
6. *Ibid.*, p. 20.
7. *Centenary Volume*, p. 474.
8. Vivekananda, S., *C.W.* (1984), Vol. I, p. 25.
9. *Swami Vivekananda on India and Her Problems*, p. 57.
10. *Ibid.*, p. 58.
11. Vivekananda, S., *C.W.* Vol. III, p. 242.
12. *Ibid.*, Vol. IV, p. 358.
13. *Swami Vivekananda on India and Her Problems*, p. 71.
14. Vivekananda, S., *C.F.* p. 303.
15. *Ibid.*, p. 232.
16. *Ibid.*, Vol. III, p. 242.
17. *Ibid.*, Vol. I, p. 124.
18. *Ibid.*, Vol. IV, p. 415.
19. *Swami Vivekananda on India and Her Problems*, p. 100.
20. *Ibid.*, p. 101.
21. Vivekanada, S., *C.W.*, p. 321.
22. *Ibid.*, Vol. IV, p. 358.
23. *Ibid.*, Vol. V, p. 45.

4

Sri Aurobindo's Philosophy of Education

Among the contemporary Indian philosophers of education Sri Aurobindo occupies a very important position particularly due to his wide knowledge of Eastern and Western, ancient and modern systems of education and principles of educational psychology. He presents an integral philosophy of education. His *Asram* at Pondicherry has, therefore, grown into an important place of learning. Here experiments are even now being conducted to evolve a new system of education particularly valuable from the point of view of evolution of man.

Analysis of Human Nature

Field of Human Personality

Man, according to Sri Aurobindo, should be looked not only in vertical but also in horizontal perspective. His is an inter-disciplinary approach to the problem of the analysis of human nature. His perspective is integral as far as possible. He tries to supply the missing links in the studies of human personality by psychology, sociology, anthropology and biology. Man, according to him, is a micro-cosm in macrocosm. As he puts it, "Society is only an enlargement of the individual."[1] Man's personality has a triple perspective— individuality, universality and transcendence. Sri Aurobindo emphasises both the aspects of human experience. He adds new dimensions to the distinction between men and animal. He said, "Man, the mental being in Nature, is specially distinguished from her less developed creatures by a greater power of individuality, by the liberation of the mental consciousness which enables him finally to understand more and more himself and his law of being and his development, by the liberation of the universal will which enables him under the secret control of the universal will to manage more and more the materials and lines of his development and by the capacity in the end to go beyond himself, beyond his mentality and open his consciousness into that from which mind, life and body proceed."[2] As distinguished from the animal, man has not only superior capacities but also immense possibilities. It is so because man has in him a principle transcending his limited physical, vital and mental being. It is precisely on this principle that Sri Aurobindo based his system of education. This fact distinguishes his philosophy of education from other contemporary Indian educational philosophies.

Man, according to Sri Aurobindo is a nodes in an infinite non-individual as well as super-individual field. In his own words, "The individual is a centre of the whole universal consciousness."[3] This universal field constantly acts and reacts upon man. The destiny of man is not only shaped by the universal cause. To quote Sri Aurobindo, "The Master and Mover of our works is the One, the Universal and Supreme, the Eternal and the Infinite .... All that is—is He, and He is more than all that is, and we ourselves, though we know it not, are being of his being, force of his force, conscious with a consciousness derived from his; even our mortal existence is made out of his substance and there is an immortal within us that is a spark of the Light and Bliss that are forever."[4] Thus, in analysing human nature, Sri Aurobindo goes beyond man to point out the supra-mental forces working upon him. Man, according to him, is a transitional phase in the evolution of nature which aims at super-man. The aim of education, therefore, is not only the all round development of man but also his evolution towards super-man. This, however, will be done not by education but through *Yoga*.[5]

Structure of Human Personality

Through this Yogic psychology, Sri Aurobindo goes deeper into the recesses of human consciousness and unravels new faculties, processes and forces. Man according to him is, "A spirit using the mind, life and body for an individual and a communal experience and self-manifestation in the universe."[6] The inner structure of man is made of the self or spirit, the soul and the psychic being, the physical, the vital, the mental and psychical and the spiritual sheaths or bodies which enclose the physical body and the ego. Except the ego all these are the projections of the self for its manifestation on the earth. The mental being is concerned with, "Cognition and intelligence, with ideas, with mental or thought perceptions, the reaction of thought to things, with the truly mental movements and formations, mental vision and will, etc., that are part of his intelligence."[7] The vital being "is the life nature made up of desires, sensations, feelings, passions, energies of action, will of desire, reactions of the desire-soul in man and of all that play of possessive and other related instincts, anger, fear, greed, lust, etc., that belong to this field of nature."[8]

Double Soul

The soul again, is double. There is a surface desire soul and the subliminal psychic entity. This psychic entity is the real soul or *Caita Purusa*. This is the *jivatman*, the self, the universal man.

Five Sheaths

The soul is enclosed in five sheaths—physical, vital, mental, psychical and the spiritual. Of these, the last two correspond to the psychic being and spirit. All the five sheaths have double aspects, the surface and the inner. Thus, there is a surface physical, vital, mental, psychical and spiritual. "The surface vital is narrow, ignorant, limited, full of obscure desires, passions, cravings, revolts, pleasures and pains, the transient joys and griefs, exaltations and depressions. The true vital being, on the contrary, is wide, calm, strong, without limitations, firm and immovable, capable of all power, all knowledge, all *Ananda*. It is moreover without ego, for it knows itself to be, a projection and instrument of the Divine. In the same way there is, too, a true mental being, a true physical being. When these are manifest, then you are aware of a double existence in you: that behind is always calm and strong, that on the surface alone is troubled and obscure."[9]

Seven Cakras

These bodies possess seven main centers known as *Cakras*. These are located at the base of the spine, over the solar plexus, the spleen, the heart, in front of the throat, between the eye brows and over the top of the head.

Levels of Consciousness

In analysing the human nature Sri Aurobindo points out to different levels of consciousness. Besides the conscient level there is the inconscient, the sub-conscient, the super-conscient and the subliminal. The sub-conscient includes the unconscious as analysed by Frend and Jung. It is a very valuable level for the integration of human personality. It is indispensable for the transformation of human nature. According to Sri Aurobindo, "It sustains and reinforces all in us that clings most and refuses to change, our mechanical recurrences of unintelligent thought, our persistent obstinacies of feeling, sensation, impulse, propensity, our uncontrolled fixities of character."[10]

Aims of Education

The philosophy of education propounded by Sri Aurobindo is based upon certain fundamental principles. The aims of education follow from these principles. These principles are triple, as follows:

First, the child should himself know and develop, the teacher should only guide and help. This is true for every one without distinction of age and sex.

Secondly, education must suit the particular qualities, capacities, ideas and virtues, etc., of the person concerned. The second principle, in the words of Sri Aurobindo is, "That the mind has to be consulted in its own growth."[11] There should be no imitation. Each individual and each community should have a system of education suitable to its nature. Everywhere the basic principle is to follow one's own *Svadharma*. The aim of education is self-realisation in the individual as well as in the community. Education should help the growing soul to draw out what is best in itself and to make it perfect. To quote Sri Aurobindo, "The closer touch attempted with the psychical being behind the vital and physical mentality and an ever-increasing reliance on its possibilities must lead to the ultimate discovery that man is inwardly a soul and a conscious power of the Divine and that the evocation of this real man within is the right object of education and indeed of all human life, if it would find and live according to the hidden truth and deepest law of its own being."[12]

"The third principle of education", according to Sri Aurobindo, "is to work from the near to the far, from that which is to that which shall be."[13] This is a corollary of the second. Everything should be natural to the student, not only the aim but also the means of education. The national system of education should be rooted in the national language. This, however, does not imply any antagonism to foreign languages. According to Sri Aurobindo, "The aim and principle of a true national education is not certainly to ignore modern truth and knowledge but to take our foundation on our own belief, our own mind, our own spirit."[14]

"The chief aim of education", said Sri Aurobindo, "should be to help the growing soul to draw out that in itself which is best and make it perfect for a noble use."[15] This aim of education, as defined by Sri Aurobindo, agrees with the definitions of the aim of education advanced by most of the important philosophers of education in East and West. Education, according to Sri Aurobindo, is always self-education. It is a process to realise the inner nature of the educand. As he put it, "The child's education, ought to be an upbringing of all that is best, most powerful, most intimate and living in his nature; the mould into which the man's action and development ought to run is that of his innate quality and power. He must acquire new things but he will acquire them best, most vitally on the basis of his own developed type and inborn forces."[16] In the process of education the educand uses the different elements of education to realise his own nature. Thus, education, according to Sri Aurobindo is *paido-centric*.

Means of Education

This education, has not to do something new, but to manifest and develop the potentialities of the human being. As Sri Aurobindo said, "Nothing can be taught to the mind which is not already concealed as potential knowledge in the unfolding soul of the creature."[17] Again, "The true basis of education is the study of the human mind, infant, adolescent and adult."[18] Thus, Sri Aurobindo does not accept extreme environmentalism. Means of education, according to him, should be developed according to human nature. The means of education are determined not only by the psychology of the human individual but also that of human society.

The instrument of education, according to Sri Aurobindo, is the mind or *Antahkaran*, *Antahkaran* according to Sri Aurobindo, consists of the following four layers.[19]

(i) ***Citta***: This is the reservoir of past memories and mental impressions. This has two aspects, passive and active, with passive and active memory, respectively. It is the latter which needs education and training.

(ii) ***Manas***: This receives images of things through sensations by different sense-organs. It also directly receives mental images and forms mental impressions. These sensations and impressions supply material to thought. Thus, the training of sense organs and organs of activity is a prelude to all sound thinking and the first step in a proper education.

(iii) ***Buddhi***: This is the instrument of thought. It systematises sensations, images and mental impressions. Its functions are of two types as follows:

(a) Functions and faculties of the right hand: These include judgment, imagination, memory and observation. Its abilities are comprehensive, creative and synthetic. This part of the mind is the master of knowledge. It penetrates the soul. It grasps that which is elusive and unascertained. Its abilities act and manipulate in their own right.

(b) Functions and faculties of the left hand: These are critical and analytic and include comparison and reasoning. The critical abilities are the component parts of the logical reason. They perform the functions of distinction, comparison, classification, generalization, deduction, inference and conclusion. This part of the mind follows the ascertained truths. It touches only the body of knowledge. Both the above mentioned types of functions and abilities are essential for the working of human reason. Hence, both require proper training and development in a sound system of education.

(iv) ***Supra-normal faculties***: These comprise of the functions included in the working of phenomena such as ESP (Extra-Sensory Perception) including telepathy and clairvoyance and PK (psycho kinesis) and the phenornena of genius. These, however, cannot be developed by instruction. The educator can only remove the impediments in their growth. He should see that they develop properly and without hindrances. Sri Aurobindo has not only emphasized the importance of these supra-normal or para-normal functions, he has also given hints for their control in his yogic writings.[20]

Types of Education

The types of education in a particular philosophy, directly follow from the aim of education. As Sri Aurobindo's philosophy of education aims at an all round drawing out of what is best in a child, the types of education, according to him, include the education of the senses, education of body, education of the mind and also the moral education and the religious education. Thus, all the types of education find a place in the scheme of education as visualised by Sri Aurobindo. He is against teaching by snippets. He does not favour introduction of several subjects at the early stage. This should be only after a person thoroughly masters one or two subjects. This builds up a deeper and nobler culture. Education should start at the age of 7 or 8 years when the child is fairly capable of concentration so that he may attend a subject for a sufficiently long time. The child should be made interested in his subject, "To lead him on step by step, interesting and absorbing him in each -as it comes, until he has mastered his subject, is the true art of teaching."[21]

The Education of the Senses

The most important type of the early education of the child is the training of his senses. The child gathers the materials for his mental development through his senses of sight, hearing, touch, smell and taste, etc. These sense organs function through the physical nerves and their organs such as eyes, ears, nose, skin and pallet. The training of senses means the perfection of the senses in their functions. This involves accuracy and sensitiveness. This depends upon unobstructed activity of the nerves and the openness of the mind. The sense organs should be healthy so that they may conduct their functions with perfect ease. Therefore, the educationist should he cautions against the defects of the physical organs and get them examined and cured by the physician. Besides the defects of the sense organs, another source of difficulty in the functioning of the senses is the nervous obstruction. This may be of two types—firstly, the obstruction which stops information reaching the mind and secondly, the obstruction which distorts the information. To remove the obstruction of the senses Sri Aurobindo, in the tradition of *Yoga,* suggests *Nadisuddhi, i.e.*, the regulation of breathing. This helps in quietening of the nervous system and remedying the emotional difficulties.

Besides the obstruction of the nerves, another source of disturbance in the functioning of the senses is the obstruction in the mind or *manas. Manas*, according to Sri Aurobindo, is both a sense organ as well as a channel. Its obstruction acts in both these forms. In the first form it can be improved by sense training. In the second form the obstructions are mainly due to some obstacles. Sri Aurobindo has classified these obstacles into the following types:

1. ***The nervous emotional obstructions***: These obstructions are partly nervous and partly emotional. These can be removed by purification of the nervous system.
2. ***Emotion warping by impressions***: This type of obstacle can be removed by the purification of moral habits. Thus, moral education has an important place in Sri Aurobindo's system of education.
3. ***Interference of previous associations***: These associations are formed in the *Citta*. These can be removed by what is known as *Citta Suddhi* or purification of mental and moral habits in the *Citta*. In the words of Sri Aurobindo, "It consists in bringing about passivity of the restless flow of thought sensations rising of its own momentum from the passive memory independent of our will and control."[22] The *Citta Suddhi* purifies the intellect and removes prejudices and pre-conceptions. After *Citta Suddhi* the intellect can adequately discriminate, choose, select and arrange.

Education of Mind

While the first type of child's education is the training of the senses, the second is the training of mind. This requires development of intellect, which in its turn comes after concentration of attention. Concentration is easy if the object is interesting. Steady and natural long practice leads to the development of the power of double, triple or multiple concentration. This is known as *Abhyas*. This different type of concentration is necessary for the attainment of knowledge. Besides development concentration, muscular coordination, particularly the co-ordination of the hands with the sense organs is a necessary part of early mental training. According to Sri Aurobindo, "Imitation by the hand ensures accuracy of observation."[23] This is particularly explicit in the case of child's learning of drawing. Like Froebel, Sri Aurobindo lays emphasis upon learning through activity. He, however, also emphasises learning through passivity. While the child should learn through the activity of his senses and physical organs, he should also practice to make his mind passive and receptive so that it may be opened to the knowledge around him. This makes Sri Aurobindo's educational psychology quite comprehensive.

In the attainment of knowledge as required in education of the mind Sri Aurobindo points out that while mastering a particular subject the appeal to the particular traits of the mind is more necessary than mere presentation of date concerning different fields of knowledge. Thus, history can be taught by appealing to interesting narratives, hero worship and patriotism. The teaching of science can be improved by appealing to the child's tendencies to inquire, investigate and analyse. Teaching of philosophy is helped by the arousal of child's curiosity and by turning it to metaphysical enquiry. The teaching of art requires an appeal to the child's gift of imitation and imagination. Similar is the case with other subjects. Everywhere the presentation of data should go along with arousal of mental tendencies.

Like other yogic-teachers Sri Aurobindo lays emphasis upon concentration in the attainment of knowledge. According to him, "The first thing the teacher has to do is to accustom the pupil to concentrate attention."[24] In the training of concentration again, the proper sequence is first concentration upon things and after it concentration upon word and finally upon ideas. The observations again, should be multi-sided and comprehensive. The child should know a thing through all his senses, analyse it and observe it attentively, succinctly, and systematically. This process should go on till he knows the object as a whole. This should, however, not require any pressure from the teacher or the environment. Learning, according to Sri Aurobindo, should be always spontaneous, then alone it may be effective.

After the achievement of concentration of attention the teacher should encourage memory and judgment in the child. The training of the memory should not be through mechanical repetition but by the use of natural things such as flowers, etc. The child may be encouraged to observe distinctions among the objects of senses and compares and contrasts them. The comparison and contrast of the flowers, leaves, plants and trees is a sound foundation for the knowledge of Botany. Similarly in other subjects also learning may be helped by the use of observation. For example, Astronomy may be learnt by the observation of stars. Geology may be learnt by the observation of the earth and stones. Entomology may be studied by the observation of insects and Zoology by the observation of animals. Sri Aurobindo's statements here are in agreement with other contemporary philosophers of education in East and West. Thus, observation is the basis for the education of science. In the words of Sri Aurobindo, "There is no scientific subject the perfect and natural mastery of which cannot be prepared in early childhood by this training of the faculties to observe, compare, remember and judge various classes of objects."[25]

Besides concentration and observation the education of the mind requires training of the judgment. In this field the first requirement is self-confidence so that the child may trust his judgment. Besides self-confidence the child should be able to compare his judgment with those of others so that he may discover his mistakes.

Moral Education

Moral education occupies an important place in Sri Aurobindo's system of education. It means the training of moral faculty, i.e., the ability to distinguish between what is right and what is wrong. Sri Aurobindo has everywhere deplored the tendency to equate education with bookish knowledge. Moral text-books can at the most make a mechanical artificial moral thinking while man's moral nature includes emotions, impressions and temperament. Unless these are transformed the child cannot become moral. Without this transformation, thinking and ideas and the external actions at best touch the fringe and not the centre. Books can improve the intellect but not integrate emotions. Institutional discipline, compulsions and repressions cannot make the educand's moral. If the teacher is successful in getting the admiration of the pupils, they tend to accept his commands and follow him, then moral education should become a part of child's nature. Sri Aurobindo favours the ancient Indian system of education in which the *Guru* was the living ideal before the disciples and the latter learnt by the examples of the former. Another important thing in moral education is the value of suggestion. The suggestion by the teacher has to be exercised by personal example, daily talks and *Svadhyaya,* i.e., reading good books. Narration of the deeds of great men in an interesting style always carries much impression upon the delicate minds of young students For elder students the ideals and activities of great men should be presented in a way which may arouse deeper emotions and higher aspirations. According to Sri Aurobindo, "The wildness and recklessness of many young natures are only the over-flowing of an excessive strength, greatness and nobility. They should be purified, not discouraged."[26]

Religious Education

The essence of education, according to Sri Aurobindo, is "To live for God, for humanity, for country, for others and for oneself in these."[27] Like moral teaching religious education should also be imparted not through religious books or religious sermons, but by the practice of religious life, spiritual self-training and exercise. Theoretical teaching of religion must be complemented with actual practice. The religious practice, however, cannot have any fixed pattern for everyone. No particular form suitable to the particular individual.

Physical Education

Education, according to Sri Aurobindo, is the integral evolution of man. This includes physical education. As Sri Aurobindo puts it, "If our seeking is for a total perfection of the being, the physical part of it cannot be left aside; for the body is the material basis, the body is the instrument which we have to use."[28] The physical education aims at the perfection of the body, its health, strength and fitness. Man's individual and collective life requires certain habits, capacities and qualities which may be developed through sports and games. Physical culture keeps the body fit and strong and helps in the development of such traits as high sense of discipline, morals and high character. Different traits are needed for success in different sports and games and naturally these traits are developed by them. Marches and Drills help in the formation of a capacity for harmonious and right movement of the body. This physical culture economises physical efforts and discourages waste of energy. Physical education helps in the inculcation of sportsman-spirit, sense of discipline, obedience, order and team work. All these traits, are useful in individual and collective life. These traits, however, are only the external benefits of physical education. Sri Aurobindo has a deeper insight into the value of physical culture when he says, "The development of the utmost value is the awakening of the essential and instinctive body-consciousness which can see and do what is necessary without any indication from mental thought and which is equivalent in the body to swift insight in the mind and spontaneous and rapid decision in the will."[29]

Education of Yoga

The above discussion makes it clear that the aim of education, according to Sri Aurobindo, is man's integral evolution. This is a two-fold process. While on the one hand, it requires multi-sided growth and development, on the other hand, it also requires a gradual progress towards higher levels. It is hence that Sri Aurobindo has considered education, insufficient without *Yoga*. In other words, education, like all other types of human endeavors, is a part *Yoga*, i.e., man's attempt to integral evolution. Thus a complete education needs the help of *Yoga*. In other words, *Yoga* is the culmination of education. Both education and *Yoga* seek the same ultimate ideal of individual and social development. Where educational practices exhaust their best means for this purpose, *Yoga* takes up to lead man to perfection.

Medium of Education

Like other contemporary Indian philosophers of education including Vivekananda, Rabindra Nath, Gandhi and Dayananda, Sri Aurobindo considers the mother tongue as the best medium of instruction. It is only through one's own mother tongue that one should begin one's education. Other languages can be mastered only after a sound knowledge of one's mother tongue has been attained. The mastery of the mother tongue enables the educand to understand the literature and history of his country and the life around him. This is particularly true about the early education of the child.

Teaching Methods

The teaching methods in the integral education of Sri Aurobindo are based on the one hand on faith in the inner goodness and evolutionary nature of the educand and on the other hand on the psychological principles involved in teaching. Sri Aurobindo's explanations and suggestions are everywhere psychological. Without going into the details he has always kept his eye focused on the tendencies working within. Therefore, his suggestions are very valuable.

Teaching Children

Sri Aurobindo and The Mother gave particular attention to the methods of teaching children. In this connection the following suggestions are offered.[30]

1. The teachers should have sufficient documentation of what they know. They should be able to answer all questions.
2. They should have at least the knowledge if not the experience of true intellectual and intuitive attitude. This knowledge can be attained through mental silence.
3. He is the best teacher who has the capacity and not only knowledge of the different fields of evolution.
4. Thus, the professors must be sincere in discipline and experience. They should not be propagandists.
5. To start with, "The children, as soon as they have the capacity to think (it begins at 7 years and towards 14 years it is very clear) should be given small indications at 7 and a complete explanation at 14, of how to do it, and

that it is the unique method to enter into relation with the profound truth of things, that all the rest is a mental approximation, more or less inapt of something that can be known directly."[31]

Teaching Very Small Children

About the teaching of very small children, The Mother has, laid down the following principles for the teachers:[32]

Never to deceive oneself.
Never to be angry.
Always to be understanding.
Never try to impose on them.
Never scold but always try to understand.

With Rousseau Sri Aurobindo believes that the child is naturally good but gradually corrupted by bad environment. In an adverse environment the child looses all contact with the inner guide, the self in him. Therefore, The Mother has insisted that the most necessary thing to be taught to the child is to follow the inner psychic consciousness. As she said, "That is why I insist on that and I say that from the very earliest age children must be taught that there is a reality within—within themselves, within the earth, within the universe exist only as a function of this truth and if it did not exist, he would not last, even the short time he lasts and that everything would dissolve as soon as it is created.[33]

This, however, does not require philosophical explanations. The child is not prepared for mental understanding of the self. He should be made to realise the inner consciousness. His education, therefore, should be by projects and play way method. The child responses to the psychic vibrations. He is most impressed by affection and feelings. Therefore, integral education rules out all harsh treatment, scolding or being angry towards the children. One must have sufficient patience with them. The habits for cleanliness and hygiene should start very early. This, however, does not require creating fear of illness in the child. The Mother has warned, "Fear is the worst, inceptive for education and the surest way of attracting what is feared."[34] This warning is timely not only for early education but for secondary and university education in our country.

How to Teach

Sri Aurobindo, in his exposition of teaching methods, keeps his eye focused on the truth alone. He is neither prejudiced in favour nor against the ancient Indian teaching methods or the Western ways of teaching. As he said, "The past hangs about our necks with all its prejudices and errors and will not leave us; it enters into our most radical attempts to return to the guidance of the all-wise Mother. We must have the courage to take up clearer knowledge and apply it fearlessly in the interest of posterity."[35]

Successive Teaching

Accepting that every child has multiple tendencies and abilities requiring teaching of various subjects, Sri Aurobindo favours successive teaching as against simultaneous introduction of so many subjects to be taught to the child. The basic subject should be introduced first so that a sound foundation for education is made. As Sri Aurobindo points out, "The old system was to teach one or two subjects well and thoroughly and then proceed to others and certainly it was a more rational system than the modern. If it did not impart so much varied information, it built up a deeper, nobler and more real culture."[36] Thus, different subjects should be studied one by one. The same principle is applicable to the teaching of text books. Each chapter should be studied thoroughly and in succession. In the words of The Mother, "One should leave a chapter when it has been fully grasped, then only take up the next one and so on. And if a chapter is finished, it is finished: and if it is not finished, it is not finished."[37] The child's education should start at the age of 7 or 8 for, according to Sri Aurobindo, "That is the earliest permissible age for the commencement of any regular kind of study."[38] At this age the child is capable of concentration and interest. Therefore, the first thing to be created in the child is interest in the subject.

Education through Practical Experience

Thus, like all other modern educators Sri Aurobindo pleads for introducing of different subjects to the child through practical experience. First of all he should acquire mastery of the mother tongue as the medium of the education, because that is the required sound basis for regular instruction. Elaborating the need of practical foundation of child's education. Sri Aurobindo gives valuable suggestions for the teaching of different subjects appealing to the imagination, the dramatic faculty, love for the narrative, hero worship, urge to enquiry and other natural characteristics of the child. To quote his advice, Almost every child has an imagination, an instinct for words, a dramatic faculty, a wealth of idea and fancy. These should be interested in the literature and history of the nation. Instead of stupid and dry spelling and reading books, looked on as a dreary and ungrateful task, he should be introduced by rapidly progressive stages to the most interesting parts of his own literature and the life around him and behind him, and they should be put before him in such a way as to attract and appeal to the qualities of which I have spoken. All other study at this period should be devoted to the perfection of the mental functions and the moral character. A foundation should be laid at this time for the study of history, science, philosophy, art, but not in an obtrusive and formal manner. Every child is a lover of interesting narrative, a hero-worshipper and a patriot. Appeal to these qualities in him and through them let him master without knowing it the living and human parts of his nation's history. Every child is an inquirer, an investigator, analyser, a merciless anatomist. Appeal to those qualities in him and let him acquire without knowing it the right temper and the necessary fundamental knowledge of the scientist. Every child has an insatiable intellectual curiosity and turn for metaphysical inquiry. Use it to draw him on slowly to an understanding of the world and himself. Every child has the gift of imitation and a touch of imaginative power. Use it to give him the ground work of the faculty of the artist."[39]

All this should be done informally. One should avoid set rules of teaching and memorising. Sri Aurobindo is everywhere against mechanical processes of teaching. The teaching should first arouse the interest of the child and then depend upon spontaneous use of his abilities. The child should be allowed absolute freedom in his progress.

Free Progress System

The followers of Sri Aurobindo have developed a free progress system of education, whose salient features are as follows:[40]

1. The structure is oriented towards individual needs, interests and abilities.
2. The aspiration, experience of freedom, self-education and experimentation relating inner needs with the curricular provisions, discovering the higher lines of life and the art of living are the important aspects which this system tries to encompass.
3. Each student is free to study any subject he chooses at any given time under a sympathetic guidance.
4. Promotion of individual endeavor.
5. Weekly announcement of time table and lectures to be delivered.
6. Promotion of discussion between teachers and taught and between taught and taught.
7. Projects are announced in each subject and the students select according to their choice.

Education for Different Sections of Society

In his system of education, Sri Aurobindo does not make any distinction in different sections of society on the basis of sex, caste, class, race, etc. The education for man and woman should be similar in all respects. Clarifying this rejection of sex distinctions in education. The Mother said, "What we claim is this, that in similar conditions, with the same education and the same possibilities, there is no reason to make a categorical distinction, final and imperative between what we call men and women. For us human beings are the expression of a single soul."[41] In his interpretation of his ancient social system Sri Aurobindo laid emphasis upon equality of sexes. He lamented that later on women were subjugated to men leading to degeneration of society. He proposes that the women should be everywhere treated as equals to men. He is against the ancient Indian psychological dictum that male and female should avoid each other's company. He, on the other hand, maintains, "There is no impossibility of friendship between man and woman pure of this element (sex), such friendships can exist and have always existed. All that is needed is that the lower vital should not look in at the back door or be permitted to enter."[42] Therefore, no distinctions are made between boys and girls in The Mother's

International School or Sri Aurobindo International University at Pondicherry. The most unique feature of the education at these two institutions is the prescription of physical exercises both for boys and girls. Clarifying this policy The Mother said, "In all cases, as well for boys as for girls, the exercises must be graded according to the strength and capacity of each one. If a weak student tries at once to do hard and heavy exercises, he may suffer for his foolishness. But with a wise and progressive training girls as well as boys can participate in all kinds of sports and thus, increase their strength and health."[43] According to Sri Aurobindo both men and women are equally capable to evolve towards perfection to reach Gnostic age.

Critical Remarks

Sri Aurobindo has, however, not given an attention to the education of the backward, economic and social classes in society. Here M.K. Gandhi was more integral. Social integration requires that special attention is given to those sections which are lagging behind.

The Humanist Problem

From the purely humanistic viewpoint, one arrives at some grave difficulties in Sri Aurobindo's philosophy of education. The ultimate goal according to him, is not man but superman. Admitted that he has accepted the possibility of the evolution of man himself to super-man but in this process the human values, the human warmth and intimacy may be lost. The very idea of divinization of man may appear to some as a *utopia* or even something foreign to human nature. The supra- mental knowledge, which has been accepted as the goal of human knowledge may not be acceptable to those according to whom man's bliss lies not in the achievements of knowledge as such but in more and more progress towards it. It is undeniable that the Infinite is valuable but the value of education lies in the finite element in man. Thus, Sri Aurobindo's philosophy of education cannot be called humanistic. This, however, does not mean that it stays lower than the human ideal, in fact it rises above it by accepting the supra-mental life as fulfillment of body, life and mind. Sri Aurobindo has pointed out to a higher more harmonious and integral type of human life.

Integral Approach

The most significant contribution made by Sri Aurobindo to the world of education is his integral approach. Today human beings everywhere suffer from one-sidedness in thought and action. The days of 'isms' in philosophy of education are over. In the beginning of the present century there were 'isms' in different fields of thought including philosophy, psychology and education. Scholars were classified into different schools. Today, inter-disciplinary studies have shown that all human sciences are closely connected among themselves and also with philosophy. The most significant truth that has emerged in the present day knowledge is that reality is multi-sided. The most important fact about human nature is that it is many-faceted, complex and involves individual differences. Sociology has shown the importance of social factors in the field of education. Social anthropology has shown that man is more a cultural than a biological being. Thus, innumerable factors, influence the modern child. Therefore, integral approach is the truth of our time. It is the most important single message of Sri Aurobindo. The key to understand his thought in education, is the integral approach. As has been already pointed out, his explanation of development is integral including physical, vital, mental, religious, moral and spiritual education. Education aims at perfection. This perfection, according to Sri Aurobindo, requires a development of all the aspects of human personality, cognitive, conative and affective. As he said, man becomes perfect "when he combines in himself the idealist and pragmatist, the originative soul and the executive power."[44]

Spiritual Ideal of Education

Sri Aurobindo aims at the evolution of a spiritual individual, community and humanity. This was the ideal of his *yoga* which is the end of the whole life. In his philosophy of history he traces the evolution of human society through various stages and predicts the future spiritual evolution of man. Thus, his education is future-oriented. It does not only meet the present needs of individual and society but also aims at the descent of Gnostic consciousness upon earth. It aims at fulfillment of body, life and mind and also a spiritual transformation of all these. It aims not only at change but also at total transformation. Thus, it suffers from perfectionist bias. It may be pointed out that if our aim in education is too high, there is a danger of falling too low. That is why in spite of all talk about allowing more and more freedom in education, a necessary condition for spiritual evolution, most of the Governments in progressive countries are still exercising more and more control on education. Abolition of state control is still a far cry. Withering of the state, to borrow a phrase from Karl Marx is still a *utopia*. However, the criteria of judging a philosophy is the consistency of thought and not always immediate practical success. It is here that Sri Aurobindo's philosophy of education presents its credentials to reason. The spiritual ideal of the individual and society is an aim cherished by great thinkers from Plato to Sri Aurobindo. The dream may not come true but still the game is worth the candle.

References

1. Aurobindo, S., *The Human Cycle* (New York: The Sri Aurobindo Library Inc., 1950), p. 105.
2. *Ibid.,* p. 69.
3. Aurobindo, S., *The Life Divine* (Pondicherry: Sri Aurobindo Ashram), Vol. I, 2nd ed., p. 45.
4. Aurobindo, S., *The Synthesis of Yoga* (New York: Sri Aurobindo Library Inc., 1950), p. 231.
5. Sharma, R.N., "Parapsychology and Internal *Yoga*", *Res. J. Phil. Soc. Sc.,* Vol. I, (Oct. 1963), pp. 164-177.
6. Aurobindo, S., *The Synthesis of Yoga,* pp. 717-718.
7. Aurobindo, S., *Lights on Yoga* (Pondicherry: Sri Aurobindo Ashram, 1953), pp. 22-23.
8. *Ibid.*, p. 23.
9. *Ibid.*, p. 18.
10. Aurobindo, S., *The Life Divine,* Vol. II, p. 655,
11. Aurobindo, S., *A System of National Education* (Calcutta: Arya Publishing House, 1948), pp. 3-6.
12. Aurobindo, S., *The Human Cycle,* p. 35.
13. Aurobindo, S., *A System of National Education,* p. 5.
14. Aurobindo, S., *Integral Education,* compiled by Dr. Indra Sen (Pondicherry: Sri Aurobindo International University Centre, 1952), p. 4.

15. Aurobindo, S., *A System of National Education*, p. 5.
16. Aurobindo, S., *Essays on the Gita* (Calcutta: Arya Publishing House, 1949), Second Series, p. 2.
17. Aurobindo, S., *The System of Yoga,* p. 2.
18. Aurobindo, S., *A System of National Education*, p. 1.
19. *Ibid.,* pp. 7-12.
20. Sharma, R.N., "Control of Psy-Phenomena in Sri Aurobindo's Yoga", *Indian Journal of Psychology,* Vol. III, No. 3 (1961-62), pp. 27-30.
21. *Ibid.,* p. 21.
22. *Ibid.,* p. 39.
23. *Ibid.,* p. 44.
24. *Ibid.,* p. 46.
25. *Ibid.,* p. 49.
26. Aurobindo, S., *A System of National Education*, p. 20.
27. *Ibid.,* pp. 24-25.
28. Aurobindo, S., *The Supra-mental Manifestation* (Pondicherry: Sri Aurobindo Society), Pt. II, pp. 19-21.
29. Aurobindo, S., *Bulletin of Sri Aurobindo International Centre of Education*, Vol. XII. No. 1, Feb. 1960, p. 94.
30. *Sri Aurobindo and The Mother on Education* (Pondicherry: Sri Aurobindo Society), Pt. II, pp. 19-21.
31. *Ibid.,* p. 20.
32. *Ibid.,* p. 34.
33. *Ibid.,* p. 23.
34. *Ibid.,* p. 26.
35. *Ibid.,* p. 11.
36. Aurobindo, S., *Birth Centenary Library,* Vol. 17 (1972), p. 213.
37. *Sri Aurobindo and The Mother on Education*, Pt. II, p. 17.
38. *Ibid.*
39. *Ibid.,* pp. 11-12.
40. Joshi, K., *Nav Chetna* (New Delhi: Mothers International School, 1977), pp. 5-7.
41. *Sri Aurobindo and The Mother on Women* (1978), p. 87.
42. Aurobindo, S., *Birth Centenary Library,* Vol. 23 (1970), p. 817.
43. *On Women,* (1978), p. 58.
44. *Ibid.,* p. 306.

5

Swami Dayananda's Philosophy of Education

Among the contemporary Indian philosophers of education Swami Dayananda may be called to be the greatest representative of orientalist tradition. While, he was a great supporter of *Vedas* and other holy texts, his approach everywhere was that of a rationalist. He never accepted anything without meditating upon its advantages and disadvantages. His *magnum opus Satyartha Prakash* is an eloquent testimony to his rationalism. Pointing out the object of this great work he said, "There is not the remotest idea to hurt the feelings of any person either directly or indirectly, but on the contrary, the book proposes that men should distinguish truth from falsehood. Thus, alone can the human race steadily advance on the path of happiness, since none but the pursuing of truth is the cause of the improvement of the human family."[1] These words of Dayananda express both his rationalism and humanism. It should be remembered that modern humanism is rationalism. Its sole aim is human welfare and that too on this earth here and now. As is clear by the above object of the chief work of Dayananda, he aimed at the progress of humanity on the path of happiness. Thus it was in keeping with this aim that he presented a philosophy of education, which though based upon the ancient Indian theory of education, rationally examined every problem of education and tested it on the touch stone of human welfare.

Dayananda's philosophy of education has been elaborated in the second, third, fourth and ninth Chapters of *Satyartha*

Prakash. Explaining the aim of the author in writing the book, Dayananda said, "Though the human soul possesses the capacity for ascertaining truth, yet through self-interest, obstinacy, wrong-heartedness, ignorance and the like, it is led to renounce truth and incline towards untruth. We have freed ourselves from these influences while writing this book. It is not our object to hurt anyone's susceptibilities or to injure anyone. On the other hand, our aim is to further the advancement and advance the well-being of mankind, to help (all) men in the ascertainment of what is right and to enable them to accept truth and reject falsehood. In our opinion there is no other way of elevating the human race."[2] Dayananda tried to fulfill this humanistic ideal both positively and negatively. He said, "of course, any suggestions made by persons actuated with the spirit of furthering the welfare of humanity, on being found good, well be most acceptable,"[3] on the other hand he ruthlessly criticised those who supported untruth and rejected whatever he thought to be harmful for human welfare. According to Dayananda, taking sides due to prejudices, is not only foolish and wrong but also below the dignity of man. This emphasis on human dignity is the key point in the philosophy of education of Dayananda.

Analysis of Human Nature

Philosophy of education is based upon the concept of human nature. Dayananda supported the concept of human nature expounded by the *Vedas* and the *Upanisads*. In Chapter II of *Satyartha Prakash,* while discussing the upbringing of children, Dayananda explained the psychological basis of child's education. In Chapter III the psychology of the adolescent has been discussed. According to Vedic psychology, the mind resides in the heart and relates the body with the soul. It controls the five sense organs, five motor organs, five *pranas* and the intellect. Without the purification of this mind no knowledge can be achieved. The mind can be controlled through *Yoga*. Thus, according to Dayananda, *Yoga* is an essential part of education.

Soul: The Essence of Human Nature

According to Vedic psychology, man is neither body nor mind nor sense organs but the soul. Following this ancient tradition,

Dayananda maintained that man is essentially a soul. Describing soul he wrote, "Just as it is the man that uses his sword to kill another who is punished and not the sword, similarly, it is the soul that, by the use of such instruments as the body, the bodily senses, the organs of thought, and nervous forces, does acts—good or evil—and consequently it is the soul alone that reaps the fruits thereof— joy or sorrow. The soul is not a witness of acts. It is the actual doer that reaps the fruits of deeds done. The One Incomparable Supreme Spirit alone is the Witness. It is the soul that does acts and is, therefore, naturally engrossed by them."[4]

Soul is the real cause of bondage and liberation. Explaining the means of this bondage and liberation, Dayananda wrote, "Obedience to the will of God, dissociation from sin, ignorance, bad company, evil influences and bad habits, the practice of truthfulness in speech, the promotion of public good, even-handed justice, righteousness and the advancement of knowledge, worship of God—glorification, prayer and communion— in other words, the practice of *Yoga*, study and tuition or instruction of others, and the advancement of knowledge by righteous efforts, the employment of best means towards the accomplishment of one's object, the regulation of one's conduct in the strict accordance with the dictates of even-handed justice which is righteousness, and so on are the means of obtaining emancipation, whilst the reverse of these, disobedience to the Divine Will and the like lead to bondage."[5]

Media of Soul's Knowledge: *Five Kosas*

Besides the soul the human body comprises five systems known as five *Kosas*. Accepting this traditional view, Dayananda has explained the five *Kosas* as follows:

(i) The Physical system which comprises all the tissues and fluids of the body from bone to skin. It is the gross physical body or system.

(ii) The Vital system which comprises the five great Vital or nervauric forces:

1. *Prana* or the Expiratory force which helps to draw the air out.
2. *Apana* or the Inspiratory force that helps to draw the air into the lungs.

3. *Samana* or the Solar-sympathetic force which is situated in the centre of the abdomen, and serves to carry rasa, i.e., chyle—the essence of food—and blood to all parts of the body.
4. *Udana* or the Glosso-pharngeal force which helps to draw the food down the throat into the stomach, etc., and gives rise to strength and energy.
5. *Vyana* or the Mother-muscular force which helps the soul to move or do anything—the cause of motion.

(iii) The Mento-motor system which comprises the principle of volition, the principle of individuality, and the five principles of action, viz., articulation, grasp, locomotion, reproduction and excretion.

(iv) The Mento-sensory system which comprises the principle of judgment, the principle of memory and the five principles of sensation, viz., sight, hearing, taste, smell and touch. It is through these that the soul carries on such processes, as thinking and the like.

(v) The Spirituo-emotional system which comprises love, cheerfulness, happiness—great or little. The elementary matter called *Prakriti* is the medium through which the soul entertains these feelings.

The above-mentioned five systems are the media through which the soul acquires all kinds of knowledge, carries on all the mental processes, and performs all its actions.[6]

Three States of the Soul

In the Vedic tradition, Dayananda has accepted three states or phases of the soul viz., Wakeful phase, Dreaming phase, slumbering phase or sound sleep or *susupti.* The human soul at different times lives through these different phases.

Four Kinds of Bodies

Again, in the Vedic tradition, Dayananda accepts four kinds of human bodies. He has explained them as follows:

1. The gross physical body which is seen and felt.
2. The subtle body which comprises seventeen principles: Five nervauric or vital principles five principles of sensation, and five physical principles such as *Prithivi,*

Apah, Agni, etc., in subtle form, and the principles of volition and discernment. It also accompanies the soul in all its births and deaths. It is of two kinds:

(a) Material which is derived from the fine particles or subtle matter.

(b) Spiritual or natural which comprises the natural powers and attributes of the soul. Both these remain with the soul in the state of emancipation, and it is through them that the soul enjoys the bliss of emancipation.

3. The Causal body *(Karana Sarira)* which consists of the elementary matter—*prakriti.* It is all-pervading and, therefore, common to all souls. It is through this that the soul enters into the state called sound dreamless sleep.
4. The *Turiya* body is that through which the soul is absorbed in the contemplation of the All-blissful Supreme Spirit in the state of *samadhi* (Superior condition) developed by the practice of *Yoga* and perfect concentration. The energy born of this pure body— the product of the pure influence of the superior condition—is of great service to the soul in emancipation."[7]

Thus, Mind, Intellect, *Citta* and Ego are the four faculties of the inner instrument in human psychology. The function of the mind is to will and desire. It commands the motor organs in response to the information achieved through the five sense organs. Inside the external physical body there is a subtle body. This subtle body cannot be observed from outside. In this subtle body there are five *pranas,* five sense organs, five subtle *bhutas* and mind and intellect. Thus, there are seventy elements in this subtle body. This subtle body transmigrates. It is always with the *jiva* in life and in death. It is the basis of enjoyment of pleasure in liberation. Besides, the external gross body and the inner subtle body there is a third type of body known as causal body. It is the causal body which is responsible for deep sleep. In other words, in deep sleep the *jiva* resides in the causal body. This is the same for all *jivas.* The functions of the gross body are controlled by the subtle body. The subtle body is controlled by the impressions or *samskaras.* The *samskaras* are the result of social and moral regulations. Inside the subtle body there are five *pranas* and five sense organs. These five sense organs are in the touch, vision, taste, smell and audition. The five subtle *bhutas* correspond to these five sense organs. These are known as five *tanmatras.* The sense organs can be controlled through the mind. The three *gunas—Sativa. Rajas* and *Tamas* influence both the body and the mind.

Dayananda accepted the technique of eight-fold *yoga* expounded by *Patanjali.* Mind can be controlled through the eight-fold *Patanjali Yoga.* This again is the means to realise God. The ultimate end of human life is liberation and this liberation is the result of self-realisation. Like the author of *Gita,* Dayananda emphasised synthesis of action and knowledge. Adding non-violence to the ten characteristics of the *Dharma,* Dayananda accepted eleven characteristics of *Dharma.* He laid much emphasis upon and praised *Brahmacarya.* Like other contemporary Indian philosophers of education, including Gandhi, Vivekananda, Aurobindo, etc. Dayananda considered *Brahmacarya* to be most valuable in student life. Besides *Brahmacarya* one should also practice non-violence, truth, non-theiving and non-covetousness.

Aims of Education

In Indian Vedic tradition education is that which imparts *Vidya* or the real knowledge. In this tradition Dayananda maintained that education removes ignorance and increases knowledge, culture, religiosity and self-control. This education has five characteristics, viz., provision of right knowledge, cultivation of culture increase of religiosity, increase of self-control and liberation from ignorance. Thus, it includes this-worldly and other-worldly welfare. In his book entitled *Vyavahar Bhanu*, Dayananda maintained that education is that by which man attains happiness and the good virtues of knowledge, etc., and leaves evils like ignorance. Knowledge is that by which a thing is known as it is and through which one attains virtues. It is through knowledge that one can make others happy and himself attain happiness. On the contrary, that by which things are confused and which leaves evil effects for our self and others is ignorance. In his *magnum opus Satyartha Prakash* Dayananda distinguished between knowledge and ignorance. He said, "He who realizes the nature of *Vidya*— true knowledge—and of *Avidya*—good moral life and Divine contemplation—simultaneously conquers death by virtue of *Avidya* and obtains immortality by virtue of *Vidya*."[8] The function of education is to provide this' *Vidya*. Prior to defining right knowledge or *Vidya* Dayananda pointed out the following characteristics of *Avidya* or ignorance. These have to be removed through education:

1. "The false notion that the transient world and worldly things (such as bodies) are eternal or in other words that the world of effects, that we see and feel, has always been existing and will continue to exist for ever, and that by virtue of the power of *yoga* the physical bodies of godly men become imperishable is the first kind of *Avidya* (Ignorance).
2. To regard impure things, such as lustfulness and untruthfulness, as pure is the second kind of *Avidya* (Ignorance).
3. To believe that excessive sexual indulgence is a source of happiness, whilst it really causes pain and suffering, constitutes the third variety of *Avidya* (Ignorance).
4. To consider dead material things as possessed of soul is the fourth kind of *Avidya* (Ignorance)."[9]

Education aims at removing the above mentioned fourfold ignorance or incorrect knowledge. Besides this negative aspect of the aim of education, it has a positive aspect in the provision of right knowledge. Elucidating this right knowledge in the tradition of *Vedas*, Dayananda wrote, "This four-fold incorrect knowledge is called *Avidya* or Ignorance. The reverse of it, viz., to look upon what is temporal as temporal, what is eternal as eternal, what is pure as pure, what is impure as. impure, pain as pain, pleasure as pleasure, what is soul-less as soul-less, what is soul possessing, as soul-possessing, is called *Vidya* or knowledge."[10] Distinguishing between knowledge and ignorance Dayananda wrote "That by which the true nature of things is known is called knowledge, whilst that by which the true nature of things is not revealed and, instead, a false conception of things is formed, is called Ignorance."[11]

Thus, while pointing out the aims of education, Dayananda maintained a pragmatic and practical outlook. In the Vedic tradition he considered salvation to be the aim of education but this salvation is not an extra-terrestrial goal. It includes the realisation of human perfection as an individual as well as a collectivity here on this earth. It is hence that Dayananda laid so much emphasis on right knowledge and right conduct. In the Second Chapter of his famous work *Satyartha Prakash* he wrote, "Fathers' mothers and tutors should always give their children and students good counsel and they should also advice them to imbibe their virtues but avoid their vices."[12]

Means of Education

Dayananda devoted the second chapter of his work *Satyartha Prakash* to the upbringing of the children. In this context he elaborated his educational theory about child's, education, and showed sufficient insight in the educational and psychological principles. He held that no one can achieve knowledge without the guidance of three great teachers—the father, the mother and the preceptor. Child's education starts in the family. Emphasizing the importance of family in education, Dayananda wrote, "Blessed is the family, most fortunate is the child whose parents are godly and learned." [13] Education of the child presupposes education of the parents. The mother educates the child through her immense love. The parents should present good examples before the children as the children tend to copy the parents. As soon as the child is able to understand, the mother should instruct him in refined manners. The initial teaching of language is carried on in the family through the parents. The mother should see that the child uses his tongue properly. Besides proper speech the child should also develop proper conduct. He should again be trained in manners while addressing his superiors and inferiors. And finally what is most important is that, "Parents should endeavor to inculcate in the minds of their children an intense desire for the love of knowledge, elevating company, and control of the senses."[14]

The child's education, according to Dayananda should be both positive and negative. While on the one hand efforts should be made to develop in him such qualities as truthfulness, heroism, patience and cheerfulness, the parents should also see that the children avoid useless playing, crying, laughing and wrangling and may not develop evil qualities such as jealousy and malice, etc. They should be taught not to have superstitions. They should develop a scientific outlook towards the world. Depicting the humanistic element in his philosophy of education Dayananda wanted to develop rationalism and scientific outlook in males and females right from the childhood. He was a most vehement critic of all superstitions, beliefs in ghosts and witches, etc. He even condemned astrology and accepted only that part of it which is known as astronomy.

In the Vedic tradition, Dayananda accorded a very high place to the observation of celibacy. The parents and teachers have special responsibility in this direction. They should impart sex education to the children and impress upon their minds the need of the preservation of the reproductive elements.

Reward and punishment occupy a very important place in the child's education. Admitting the psychological importance of reward and punishment Dayananda considered them to be an important part of early education. Punishment, according to him should be oral as far as possible and not corporal. Parents who do not shirk punishment grow scholarly, cultured and educated children. Dayananda supported *Mahabharata* where it has been laid down that parents and teachers who punish their wards give them nectar while those who bestow excessive love and affection give them poison. The children should be able to understand clearly as to what is to be right and what is wrong according to their parents. The child learns through the system of rewards and punishments. He repeats those acts which lead to rewards and does not commit those acts again which result in punishment. Punishment, however, should never be given with an attitude of jealousy and malice towards the child. Summarising his theory of reward and punishment as means of education Dayananda wrote, "Children should also feel pleased when reprimanded, and feel uneasy when fondled. But parents and teachers should never reprimand them out of malice or spite. Outwardly, they should keep them in awe; whilst inwardly they should be tender hearted and kind to them. Likewise they should advise them to abstain from stealing, sexual abuse, contracting habits of indolence, arrogance, drunkenness, untruthfulness, malevolence, wickedness, malice, jealousy, blind passion; and to cultivate good qualities, such as, truthfulness and virtues."[15]

Thus, Dayananda clearly laid down the means for the moral education of the children. Moral education involves the encouragement of virtues on the one hand and the discouragement of vices on the other. The parents and the teachers should themselves present high ideals. Unless they do so they will not be able to create respect for their advices in the children. The children should be taught to speak the truth and observe their words. They should never be vain. They should avoid deceitfulness, hypocrisy and ingratitude. The child should not lose his temper nor use rough language. He should avoid useless talking and speak only as much is necessary and that too in a sweet tone. He should be taught to respect his elders, stand and salute them. He should learn to behave in society, to occupy a seat according to his rank and status. He should never have malice towards anyone. He should always speak the truth. The children should obey their parents and tutors. In the matter of dress and diet they should conduct in such a way as to gain in health, strength and knowledge. Thus in brief the child, "should try to acquire virtues and shun vices; associate with the good and avoid the wicked."[16]

Types of Education

In his scheme of education Dayananda prescribed almost similar types of education for males and females. He vehemently opposed the medieval idea that the women are not worthy of studying the *Vedas*. He pointed out that if the ladies are not allowed to go through the *Vedas* then how can they be able to participate in the *yajna* and pronounce the *mantras*. Besides a general curriculum for educands from the four *Varnas*, Dayananda also prescribed some special studies for each *Varna*. He was not in favour of prescribing any work for special duty. He pointed out that only those books should be recommended for deep study which pass all scrutiny. In his own words, "Teachers should examine everything they teach to their students with the help of the above criteria; so should the students. Otherwise they can never be profound scholars. They will only be mere crammers. Teachers before teaching a book should thoroughly study it themselves and test the truth of its contents by the application of the aforesaid test. On finding it true they should teach it to their scholars, otherwise not."[17] Thus, laying down the criteria for prescribing the curriculum, Dayananda has presented the following types of education:

1. First of all comes Phonetics by Panini, parents and teachers should teach their children and pupils how to pronounce different letters in their right places, with the right amount of effort and the right agent. For example, take the letter P. The right organ to pronounce it is the lips, the proper amount of effort is what is called full and the right agent is the tongue.
2. Then comes Grammar. It includes *Astadhyayi; Dhatu-path* (Book of roots), *Ganapath* (Book of groups), *Unadikos* (Book of prefixes and suffixes, & c). Last of all comes *Mahabhasya* (Exposition of the above four books of *Panini* by *Patanjali).*[18]

After a grounding in the science of language the educands had to study books on Vedic vocabulary and philology. The *Nighantu* and *Nirukta* by *Yaska* had to be taught in six to eight months. Then they should study prosody, i.e., *Chhado-grantha* by *Pingala.* This study will enable them to master the rules of Vedic and Sanskrit verses. This should be done in four months.

After the study of literature starts the study of sciences. In this study the educands should start from *Manusmriti* and proceed to *Valmiki Ramayana,* the *Vidurniti* and other selections like this from the *Mahabharata.* Thereafter they should study the six *Sastras* commonly known as six schools of philosophy. These should be finished in two years.

The most important part of the curriculum, according to Dayananda is covered by the four *Vedas* with their four *Brahamanas* with proper accent and meanings. The *Vedas* should be taught both by example and precept. After the study of *Vedas* the students should learn the *Upavedas.* These *Upavedas* are four in numbers:

1. *Ayurveda* or Medical Science which includes works like that of *Charak*, *Susrut* and other sages.
2. *Dhanur Veda* or Science of Government which consists of two parts—civil and military. While the civil part is

the part of governing people, the military part comprises organisation of army, etc. Both these branches should be mastered in two years, while the *Ayurveda* has to be mastered in four years.

3. *Gandharva Veda* or Science of Music which includes books like *Narad Sanhita*, etc.
4. *Atharva Veda* or Science and practice of mechanical art which is also called *Silpa Vidya.*

After the study of *Upavedas* the educands should study *Jyotisa Sastra* for two years. This includes arithmetic, algebra, geometry, geography, geology and astronomy. About the span of study to master all the above-mentioned arts and sciences, Dayananda provided 20 to 21 years. In prescribing the works for study only those books have been recommended which are either divine in origin or made by *Rsis* of the above-mentioned curriculum *Vedas* come in the former class and others in the latter. Dayananda prohibited the books of all other types which do not fall in the above-mentioned classes as they may lead to a lot of confusion and wrong knowledge.

Medium of Education

In the ancient Indian tradition Dayananda favoured mother tongue and the Sanskrit language. He strongly pleaded the cause of Sanskrit as medium of all higher education. He wrote in details about the curriculum and teaching methods for learning and mastering Sanskrit. He was vehemently critical of using foreign language such as English as medium of education not only in primary but also at the highest stage. This seriously hampers any original and creative thinking. This tradition of regard for mother tongue and Sanskrit was supported by all the Indian educational philosophers after Dayananda.

Teaching Methods

Dayananda not only prescribed a detailed curriculum but also pointed out the impediments which should be avoided both by the teachers and the taught in order to achieve the aims of education. Describing these impediments in details he wrote, "Both the teachers and their scholars should avoid all those things that act as hindrances in the way of the acquisition of knowledge, such as the company of the wicked and lascivious people, contraction of bad habits (such as the use of intoxications), fornication, child-marriage, want of perfect *Brahmacarya*, want of love on the part of the rulers, parents and learned men for the dissemination of knowledge of the *Vedas* and other *Sastras*, over-eating, keeping late hours, sloth in learning, cheating, examining or being examined, or performing these duties with dishonesty, not regarding knowledge as the highest thing in the world, want of faith in *Brahmacarya* as the source of health, strength, intellect, courage, political power and wealth, leaving off the worship of one true God, and wasting time in going about from place to place for the purpose of seeing and worshipping images made of stone, and other inanimate objects, absence of the worship of the five true living gods—father, mother, teacher, altruistic teachers of humanity *(atithis)* and others great men, neglect in the performance of the duties of their Class and Order, and instead, wearing different marks of sectarian distinction of the forehead and other parts of the body, chaplets and rosaries, etc., observance of fasting days as the 11th and 13th of each month, having faith in the forgiveness of sins by pilgrimage to such sacred places, as Banaras, and by constant recitation of the names of gods and goddesses such as *Rama*, *Krisna, Narayana, Siva, Bhagvati* and *Ganesa*, indifference towards the acquisition of knowledge through the wicked advice of hypocrites, belief in the possibilities of obtaining salvation simply through hearing such books as *Puranas* and *Bhagvata* and the like and thus neglecting the study of the true philosophies and sciences, the living of good and righteous lives, the practice of *Yoga,* and communion with God—which alone can lead to eternal bliss—want of love for knowledge through greed of gold, and loafing about, etc."[19] This long list of don'ts for teachers and scholars, incidentally summarises the evils of the present system of education. Some of them have been very much in practice in our colleges and universities and have even achieved a respectable status. Dayananda was ruthless in calling a spade. He severely condemned those who were misguiding innocent people in the name of education. He almost waged a war for the cause of the education of the backward classes including women. Thus, he demanded compulsory education in India.

Ideals of the Educator and the Educand

No system of education can benefit mankind unless the educator and the educand are prepared to follow certain ideals in the process of education. Keeping this principle in view Dayananda discussed in details the ideals required to be practiced from the teacher and the taught.

Elaborating the qualifications of teachers, whether male or female, Dayananda referred to sayings of *Mahabharata.* He supported the idea that, "He alone is a wise man who is never idle nor lazy, nor affected by pleasure or pain, profit or loss, honour or dishonour, public applause or censure, has always a firm faith in *Dharma*, and cannot be tempted by sensual objects."[20] Thus, the wise teacher should practice virtue and avoid sin. He should abstain from abusing Gods, the *Vedas* or the Virtuous people. He should have unbounded faith in God. He should be able to grasp the most difficult subject in a very short time. He should devote years after years in the pursuit of knowledge and use it for the good of mankind. He should not give opinion unasked for nor should he interrupt another in his speech. He should not brood over his looses. He should be well versed in all kinds of knowledge. He should be a clever debater, able to speak on any subject. He should have a good memory and a sound logic. He should be able to give a true exposition of scriptures. His intellectual unbuilding should be in conformity with truth. When the teachers possess the above-mentioned qualities then alone they will be able to fulfill the aims of education. Dayananda not only elaborated the qualities of a good teacher but also pointed out characteristics of undesirable teachers so that one may be able to compare between the two and gain by distinction.

Dayananda accepted the view mentioned by *Mahabharata* where it has been said, "Physical mental inertia, use of intoxicants, infatuation, idle gossip, neglect of studies, vanity, and want of *Brahmacarya.* These seven vices are not to be found among students."[21] Such students can never acquire knowledge. About the qualifications of good students again, Dayananda accepted the viewpoint expressed in *Vidurniti* of *Mahabharata,* "They alone who practise virtue, subjugate their passions and never lose their reproductive element, are true *Brahmacaris* and become learned men."[22] Thus, according to Dayananda, both the teachers and the students should possess high qualities.

These high qualities can be developed through mutual inspiration. The teachers should inculcate truthfulness, self-control, gentleness and physical and mental development on the educands. They should also try to eradicate evil habits of the students. The students, on the other hand, themselves try to develop self-control, mental tranquility, thoughtfulness, diligence and love for their teachers. They should try to attain physical and mental perfection. Emphasising the aim of education as perfection of man, Dayananda wrote, "They should so exert themselves as to acquire perfect knowledge, perfect *dharma,* perfect development of body and learn to labour."[23] The above-mentioned discussion upon the qualifications of good teachers and good scholars supply criteria for the selection of suitable teachers and suitable students in educational institutions.

Value of Brahmacarya

In his philosophy of education, Dayananda everywhere laid emphasis upon the value of *Brahmacarya* both for the teachers and the students, male and female. He supports the idea of *Manu* where it has been said, "A student should observe *Brahmacarya* and study the *Vedas* with their subsidiary subjects for 9, 18. 36 years or until they are completely mastered."[24] He classifies *Brahmacarya* into the following three grades: —

1. *The lowest*—The shortest period for observance of *Bahmacarya* for a student is 24 years.
2. *The intermediate*—The highest *Brahmacari* is he who remains a celibate for 48 years and by virtue of this acquires "perfect knowledge, perfect physical strength, perfect wisdom, perfect development of good qualities, nature and characteristics, shines like the sun, enlightening all, and is enable to master all kinds of knowledge."[25]

Thus, the aim of *Brahmacarya*, according to Dayananda, is the attainment of all round perfection of man. In India, since *Vedas,* it has been held by thoughtful persons that *Brahmacarya* is the surest way to attain perfection in human life. This view was later on supported by almost all contemporary

Indian, philosophers of education, including Vivekananda, Sri Aurobindo, Rabindra Nath and Gandhi.

Education for Different Sections of Society

While defining education as the means of individual's salvation, Dayananda also laid emphasis on its social aspect. Education aims not only on development of the personality of the educand but also on creating such man and woman in society. Dayananda did not restrict education to a certain class. He pleaded for universal education. He elaborately discussed the education of the backward classes and women. It is significant to note that according to some Vedic scholars the Sudras and the woman have no right to same type of education which is given to the higher classes of males. As a true humanist Dayananda contradicted this interpretation of Vedic: education and strongly emphasised that education must be given to everyone without distinction of class or sex. He argued in details in favour of the female education and emphasised its need right from the beginning. According to Dayananda the women should be educated not only in home science but also in grammar, religion, medicine, mathematics, and even in technology. Like the boys the girls also should be sent to residential educational institutions at the early age of eight.

Critical Remarks

Education for Perfection

The discussion of the philosophy of education presented by Dayananda leads one to the conclusion that his aim was education for perfection. He sought this aim most vigorously even sometimes presenting schemes which were far from practicable and demanding standards and virtues which could not be attained even by the selected persons. His ideas about educational institutions, segregation of male and female schools and colleges, *Gurukul* system of education, long years of *Brahmacarya* and high qualities of teachers and scholars may appear impractical to some and too rigorous to others. Undoubtedly some of his ideas, like the condemnation, of co-education and absolute segregation of male and female institutions may not be acceptable to modern educational psychologists. Some of his other ideals like the extension of the period of study to 21 years and including almost every subject on earth in his ideal curriculum may also not be acceptable to modern educationists. But these shortcomings in Dayananda's system of education should be seen in the context that he was supporting Vedic philosophy of education with all its advantages and disadvantages. He supported this system not because of its popular prestige or traditional nature but because, according to him it alone could lead to the creation of perfect men and women. Thus everywhere he sought an education for perfection. He supported democratic type of organisation in educational institutions. In the different spheres of education he was a vehement critic of all evils, sloth and degradation. He demanded very high standard of character and conduct. He wanted to realise all round perfection.

A perusal of the curriculum given in *Satyartha Prakash* amply clarifies the fact that Dayananda aimed at perfection of man through education. It is due to his anxiety about achieving an all round and most comprehensive perfection of man that he prescribed such a detailed curriculum which may appear too wide in the modern age of specialisation and yet if one remembers the fact that specialised knowledge always creates a one sided personality and never a total perfection, one may be able to appreciate Dayananda's standpoint. This, however, does not mean that such a wide curriculum may be practically taught to every person. It is undeniable that the scheme of education presented by Dayananda is too rigorous and beyond the capacity of most of the males and females in the present time. He has divided the life of human body in four stages: the period of adolescence from sixteen to the twenty-fifth years, period of manhood from twenty-fifth to fortieth years, then period of maturity after fortieth years and the period of loss after forty-eight year. Of these the first two are the stages for education. Thus a person may continue his study up to fortieth year and according to Dayananda, "The best time for marriage, therefore, is the fortieth, or rather forty-eight year."[26] It is undeniable that at present no educationist will be prepared to accept this scheme and it is not practicable by any criteria. However, what is more important for us in the assessment of Dayananda's scheme for education, is his humanist philosophy and not its actual practicability. In devising such a long curriculum and such long years of study he was only anxious for the creation of a perfect man. This aim of education is certainly laudable though Dayananda definitely over-hit the mark.

Besides the ideal of perfection as a humanist ideal, Dayananda showed his humanistic tendency in his strong condemnation of all superstitions, unscientific beliefs, immortalities and deceptions. In his support of science and the scientific outlook, he was more positive than many contemporary positivists. He was among the foremost rationalists to emphasis upon the use of reason in every field of human life. While on the one hand, he had absolute respect for the *Vedas* whom he considered to be divine, on the other hand he advised everyone to distinguish truth and untruth, use rational criteria and accept only that which is supported by sound logic. Thus, if something appears to be out of late in his scheme of education that hardly detracts its value, since what is important is not the detailed scheme but the insight behind it.

References

1. Dayananda, S., *Satyartha Prakash,* English translation by Dr. Chiranjiva Bharadwaja, (New Delhi: Sarvadeshik Arya Pratinidhi Sabha, 1975) p. i.
2. *Ibid.* Introduction, pp. ii-iii
3. *Ibid.*
4. *Ibid.,* p. 275.
5. *Ibid.,* p. 280.
6. *Ibid.,* pp. 288-289.
7. *Ibid.,* pp. 289-290.
8. *Ibid.,* p. 273.
9. *Ibid.*
10. *Ibid.,* p. 274.
11. *Ibid.*
12. *Ibid.,* p. 29
13. *Ibid.,* Chapter II, p. 20.
14. *Ibid.,* p. 29.
15. *Ibid.,* p. 28
16. *Ibid.,* p. 29

17. *Ibid.*, Chapter III, p. 69.
18. *Ibid.*, pp. 69-70.
19. *Ibid.*, pp. 76-77.
20. *Mahabharata*, 'Vidurprajagar,' XXXII.
21. *Mahabharata*, 'Vidurprajagar,' XXXIX.
22. *Mahabharata*, Chapter on 'Vidurniti'.
23. Dayananda, S., *Satyartha Prakash*, English translation, Chapter IV, p. 126.
24. Manu, *Dharma Sastra*, iii, 1.
25. Dayananda, S., *Satyartha Prakash*, English translation, Chapter Dayananda, S., III, pp. 42-43.
26. *Ibid.*, Chapter II, p. 43.

6

M.K. Gandhi's Philosophy of Education

M.K. Gandhi has been known as the apostle of non-violence. According to him non-violence is the principle which is the special characteristic of man in the world of living beings. M.K. Gandhi applied the principle of non-violence in every field of life, social, political, economic and educational. His philosophy of education, therefore, may be called an educational philosophy of non-violence. It was rooted in the fundamental truth of life.

Aims of Education

Defining the aim of education Gandhi said, "By education I mean an all round drawing out of the best in child and man, body, mind and spirit. Literacy is not the end of education nor even the beginning. It is one of the means whereby man and women can be educated. Literacy in itself is no education."[1] It is hence that Gandhi was highly critical of the educational policy imposed by the British in India. The aim of education, according to him was self-reliance. Every educated man and woman should be able to rely upon oneself to carry on his life. Earning of one's livelihood is a part of this self-reliance. Explaining this aim of education, M.K. Gandhi said, "This education ought to be for them a kind of insurance against unemployment."[2] It is hence that he laid so much stress upon industrial training in basic education. Gandhi wanted the educator to create ideal citizens through education. Keeping in view the poverty of India, Gandhi suggested that education in this country should be craft- centred. The educand must learn manual, skill and handicraft. To Gandhi in Indian circumstances this aspect of education was more important than any other aspect.

M.K. Gandhi, however, does not under estimate the aim of education as character building. Like Rousseau he wanted to make education paido-centric. As he said, "True education is that which draws out and stimulates the spiritual, intellectual and physical faculties of the children."[3] The aim of education, therefore, is the total development of the child—physical, mental and spiritual. Character formation is more important than literacy in education. When asked as to what will be the aim of education after India achieved freedom, M.K. Gandhi replied that it would be designed to develop the character of the people. In qualities of character he laid stress upon purity in thought, word and deed. He held *Brahmacarya* essential for the students. He supported ancient Indian ideals of education as aiming upon salvation.

In defining aims of education Gandhi viewed education from a comprehensive and integral standpoint. Education that develops one aspect of a child's personality at the cost of another is narrow and one sided. Such an education was imposed by British which has been the bane of Indian society. Again, instead of limiting itself to providing the child with bits of information education should aim at developing the child's personality. Ultimately, education should guide the individual to self-realisation. Education should make the child capable of self-knowledge. This stress upon the ideal of education as self-realisation, however, does not lead to neglect of the social development of the educand. To emphasise this point Gandhi said, "I value individual freedom, but you must not forget that man is essentially a social being. He has risen to his present status by learning to adjust his individuality to the requirements of social progress."[4] Addressing the students of a college Gandhi said, "Your education, if it is a vital thing, must shed its fragrance in your surroundings. You must devote a certain portion of your time daily to serving the people around in a practical manner. You must, therefore, be prepared to take the spade, the broomstick and basket. You must become voluntary scavengers of this holy place. That would be the richest part of your education, not learning by heart literary thesis."[5]

In this way Gandhi synthesized the individual and social aims of education. He did not restrict education to the achievement of any one single aim. He looked to the process of education from various perspectives. Therefore, he assigned different aims to education at different times, so much so that sometimes they looked mutually contradictory and even self-defeating. A closer examination of all these statements of Gandhi, however, shows that these aims of education are complementary to each other. In the history of education different educationists have defined the ideals of education in different ways. Most educationists have, however, felt that the aim of education is integral development of human personality. Such was also the ideal of education formulated by Gandhi. He said, "True education is that which draws out and stimulates the spiritual, intellectual and physical faculties of children."[6] Like Vivekananda, Gandhi maintained that character formation and manual skill were equally important. On the one hand, he wanted the child to earn while he learns. Oil the other hand, he also wanted the child to develop his character. According to him the criterion of an individual's cultural development is not the width of his knowledge but his inner growth. Culture, according to him, is not an adjunct of the mind but a characteristic of the soul. The aim of education is the development of such a culture. Gandhi's plans of education laid stress upon all types of education, physical, mental, moral aesthetic and religious.

As has been already pointed out, Gandhi aimed at self-reliance through education. Therefore, he visualised a craft-centred education. Explaining his scheme of basic education as an insurance against unemployment in India, Gandhi said, "The child at the age of 14, that is, after finishing a seven year course should be discharged as an earning unit. Even now the poor people's children automatically lead a helping hand to their parents—the feeling at the back of their minds being what shall they give men to cat, if I do not work with them? That is an education in itself. Even so the State takes charge of the child at seven and returns it to the family as an earning unit. You impart education and simultaneously cut at the root of unemployment."[7] Recommending this scheme of education in the report on national education the Kothari Commission declared, "We recommend that work experience should be introduced as an integral part of all education—general or vocational. We define work-experience as participation in productive work in school, in the home, in a workshop, on a farm, in a factory or in any other productive situation."[8]

Democratic Ideals of Education

Like his contemporary Indian educationists Gandhi aimed at the evolution of democratic ideal through education. His basic plan of education amply demonstrates this fact. He aimed at an education for ideal citizenship. Education, according to him, should make children ideal members of a democratic society. The school, according to Gandhi, is itself a small democratic society in which such democratic values are imparted to the children as wide outlook, tolerance and good neighbourhood. In the miniature society of the school the child learns the virtues of sympathy, service, love, brotherhood, equality and liberty, etc. These qualities are transferred from one generation to another through education. The welfare of the individual and the nation are complementary to each other. Therefore, if the country has to progress, the future generation should develop the virtues of democratic citizenship. As Gandhi said, "A nation cannot advance without the units of which it is composed advancing, and conversely, no individual can advance without the nation of which it is a part also advancing."[9]

Moral and Spiritual Aims

All knowledge is useless without a good character. In his speeches to the students at various institutions Gandhi laid emphasis upon the moral and spiritual aims of education. Emphasizing the moral aim of education Gandhi said, "The end of all knowledge must be the building up of character."[10] Character building is the moral ideal of education. According to Gandhi that is most important in a man's life. His ideal in this connection were as much in agreement with the ancient Indian thinkers as with the contemporary Western thinkers like Emerson, Ruskin, etc. Gandhi very much admired the Indian *Gurukul* system of education and the ideal of *Brahmacarya*. According to ancient Indian ideal, education aims at liberation. This was also the aim of Gujarat *Vidyapith* established by Gandhi in 1929. Gandhi, however, defined liberation in a very wide sense, including political, social and economic liberation of all the members of society. Real freedom is spiritual freedom. To attain this freedom is the task of education. Again, education equally aims at intellectual, economic and political uplift, though its chief aim is moral and spiritual. Condemning the widespread indiscipline among the students Gandhi asked them to follow the ideal of *Brahmacarya*.

According to Indian philosophy the ultimate end of all knowledge is God realisation. This God realisation again, is the meaning of self-realisation which has been considered to be the ideal of education by most of the educational philosophers in East and West. Agreeing with this line of thinking Gandhi maintained that a student should live a life of *Sanyasi*. God realisation and self-realisation are mutually complementary, the one leads to the other. This spiritual ideal of education does not negate mundane or immediate ideals but fulfils them. In the words of Gandhi, "Self-realisation is in itself an all comprehensive ideal."[11] This ideal includes other ideals of education. With Sri Aurobindo, Gandhi believed that the ultimate aim of education is spiritual. He also agreed that spiritual growth includes physical and mental, individual and social development. Thus, he synthesised different ideals of education. In his scheme of basic education, he planned for an education suitable to present day Indian society. He pondered over the difficulties of the present day Indian society and tried to find out their solution through education. His educational philosophy is based upon ancient Indian idealism. While he did not restrict the scope of physical education his attention was mainly directed towards spiritual growth.

The Basic Education

Education for Sarvodaya

Gandhi was very much aware of the needs of the country and considered basic education as the only type of education which may lead to success. His chief aim in planning for education in

India was to fulfill the needs of the country. India is a country of villages. Most of the villagers in India cannot afford to pay for their children's education. In addition to it they require their children's assistance in their occupations. Therefore, Gandhi planned for basic education which may not be a burden upon the parents and through which the children may be able to earn to meet the expenses of education themselves, laid stress upon the importance of dignity of labour and manual skill. He was convinced that an education which prepares the young men for white collar jobs can hardly be suitable for an agricultural community. It is hence that he so much emphasized the learning of craft in his plan of basic education. In spite of all his idealism Gandhi's approach everywhere was pragmatic. He was an experimenter in every field of life. Before devising his plan of basic education he experimented upon its different aspects. For him all human truths were relative. God was the only absolute. Therefore, he tested everything before suggesting it for the education of the child. He postulated that the child should himself gather knowledge from the environment and put it in actual use in life. Like the pragmatists and instrumentalists Gandhi stressed the importance of interest and activity and the need for variety in the subjects taught to the educand.

The social philosophy of M.K. Gandhi may be termed as '*Sarvodaya*'. This was the foundation of his philosophy of education. *Sarvodaya* aims at all round development of all, without distinction of caste, creed, sex and nationality. Gandhi wanted to establish a welfare state in India which he called '*Ram Rajya*'. The ideal of *Sarvodaya* does not aim at the maximum number but maximum good of all without exceptions. While Marx aimed at the welfare of the proletariat, Gandhi aimed even at the welfare of the capitalist. According to Vinoba Bhave the important characteristics of the *Sarvodaya* society are the abolition of all monopoly, emphasis on social welfare and equal, moral, social and economic importance of honest work. There is no place for any type of exploitation in *Sarvodaya* society. No one may be forced to do a certain type of work, so much so that even the wealth capitalist cannot he forcibly snatched away. Centralization, according to Gandhi, is the chief source of social evils. *Sarvodaya* requires decentralization. Gandhi aimed at political, economic, social and all other types of decentralization. In the political held decentralization requires establishment of village *panchayets*. In the economic field it requires that wealth and money should not be allowed to be concentrated in few hands but should be distributed among all the people. Social decentralization means the abolition of all types of untouchability and social distinctions.

In order to achieve the above mentioned aims of *Sarvodaya* in India, Gandhi presented his plan of basic education. He called it *Nai Talim* (New education) because it sought to build up a new society in the country. He realised that what the country needs today is not so much higher education as the education of the masses. Therefore, he did not lay so much emphasis upon higher education.

The basic education sought to fulfill the needs of the educands in a *Sarvodaya Society*. It is hence that Gandhi planned for craft centred education with mother tongue as the medium. Literacy, according to him, is not an end but only a mean of education. Education ultimately aims at the development of both mind and body and the capacity of earning one's livelihood. The syllabi for the new education were framed in such a way so as to eliminate narrow nationalism and emphasize the ideal of *Sarvodaya.* World history was taught along with Indian history. Similarly, the syllabus included the study of fund a mental universal ethics. The cost of education was brought down by compulsory manual labour, and education was tried to be made self-sufficient as far as possible.

Pointing out the value of basic education for bringing about a silent social revolution in the country Gandhi said, "It will provide a healthy and moral basis of relationship between the city and village and thus go a long way towards eradicating some of the worst evils of the present social insecurity and poisoned relationship between the classes. It will check the progressive decay of our villages and lay the foundation of a jester social order in which there is no unnatural division between the 'haves' and the 'have-nots' and everybody is assured of a living wage and the right of freedom. And all this would be accomplished without the horrors of a bloody class war or a colossal capital expenditure such as would be involved in the mechanisation of a vast continent like India. Nor would it entail a helpless dependence on foreign imported machinery or technical skill. Lastly, by obviating the necessity for highly specialized talent, it would place the destiny of the masses, as it were in their own hands."[12]

Non-Violent Education

As has been already pointed out, Gandhi emphasised the principle of non-violence in every field of life. He considered non-violence as the characteristic human quality. He said, "Non-violence is the law of our species as violence is the law of brutes."[13] Even truth was subordinate to non-violence. Gandhi said, "One had better not speak it (truth) if one cannot do so in a gentle way."[14] To those who doubted the value of non-violence to be the principle of human social organization, Gandhi pointed out, "The fact that there are so many men still alive in the world shows that it is based not on force of arms but on the force of truth and love."[15] This principle of nonviolence, Gandhi used in every aspect of education, so much so that his theory of education may be called non-violent education. Explaining his idea he wrote, "If India has resolved to eschew violence, this system of education becomes an integral part of the discipline she has to go through. We are told that English spend millions on education. America also does so. But we forget that all wealth is obtained through exploitation. They have reduced the art of exploitation to a science, and might well give their boys the costly education they do. We cannot, will not think in terms of exploitation, and we have no alternative but this plan of education which is based on non-violence."[16] Thus, according to Gandhi, India can play her role in the community of nations only by adopting the gospel of non-violence. To quote Gandhi again, "If India also tried to build up the new society based on co-operation by means of violence . . . Good brought about through force destroyed individuality. Only when the change was effected through the persuasive power of non-violent non-co-operation (i.e. love), could the foundation of individuality be preserved and real, abiding progress be assured for the world."[17]

This principle of non-violence was the basis of Gandhi's scheme of basic education. Through this scheme he wanted to develop those qualities in future citizens of India which he considered necessary for building a non-violent society. His system of education wanted to root out exploitation and centralization in society and create a non-violent social order. In 1937, Gandhi evolved a scheme popularly known as the Wardha Scheme or Basic National Education. This Wardha Scheme was based on some principles of education which were listed by Gandhi in a paper in 1932 in Yervada Jail. These postulates were as follows:

1. Boys and girls should be taught together.
2. Their time should be mostly spent on manual work under the supervision of the teacher. Manual work should be considered as part of education.
3. Work should be entrusted to each boy and girl after ascertaining his or her inclinations.
4. The child should know the why and the wherefore of every process.
5. General knowledge should be imparted to the child as soon as it is able to understand things. This knowledge should precede literary education.
6. The hand of the child should be trained to draw geometrical figures before he learns to write, that is good handwriting should be taught from the beginning.
7. The child should learn to read before he is able to write, i.e., he should learn to recognise letters as if they were pictures and then draw their figures.
8. By this method and by word of mouth, the child should acquire much knowledge before he is eight years old.
9. Children should not be compelled to learn anything.
10. The child should be interested in whatever he learns.
11. The process of teaching should be conducted in a play way, for play is an essential part of education.
12. All education should be imparted through the mother tongue of the child.
13. Every Indian child should learn Hindi-Urdu (i.e. Hindustani) as a national language before his literary training commences.
14. The second stage of the child's education begins when he is eleven and lasts up to sixteen.

15. Manual labour has a place in education during this period also. The time for literary training should be increased according to need.
16. The child should learn some vocation as preparation for his future life.
17. He should acquire a general knowledge of World History, Geography, Botany, Astronomy, Arithmetic, Geometry and Algebra.
18. A boy or a girl of sixteen years should know sewing and cooking.
19. In the third stage which begins at sixteen and end at twenty-five, a young man or woman should receive education according to his or her desire and circumstances.
20. The education commencing at the age of nine should be self-supporting. The student, while he is learning, should be engaged in such a vocation that its produce may meet the expenses of the school.
21. Production should, no doubt, begin right from the start. But it may not be enough to meet the expenses during the initial years.
22. Teachers cannot possibly have big salaries, but they must get enough to maintain themselves. They should be animated by a spirit of service. They must have a good character.
23. Huge and costly buildings are not necessary for education.
24. English can and should have a place in the syllabus only as a language. Just as Hindi is our *lingua franca*, English is a language of international inter-course and commerce.[18]

On 23rd October, 1937, a conference was organised at Wardha to finalise the basic system of education. This conference resolved that the children should be provided free education for seven years. Mother tongue should be the medium of education. Every educand must be taught some basic craft. The expenses of education should be met by the sale of the production in the school. In order to implement these recommendations a committee was formed under the chairmanship of Dr. Zakir

Hussain. This committee highlighted the basic principles, aims and organisation of basic education in its first report on 2nd December, 1937. In its second report in 1940 this committee reviewed the curriculum of basic education. Its recommendations were accepted by Indian National Congress in its session at Haripura. After Zakir Hussain Committee, another committee was formed under the chairmanship of B.G. Kher to review basic education. This committee connected it to Sergeant scheme. In the final form, the basic principles of Gandhi's scheme of primary education were: compulsory free education, education through craft, education through mother tongue, self-reliance, education connected with the life of the educand and finally inculcation of the ideals of democratic citizenship. A booklet was published by Government of India to popularise Gandhian system of education entitled *Understanding of Basic Education*. This booklet thus summarised the scheme of basic education, "Activities involving personal and community cleanliness are the foremost in a basic school. Education for the young is not stuffing impractical ideas into the minds of children. It is essentially training them in good habits, the daily experiences that every child has to undergo as regular morning evacuation, cleaning the teeth, nose and eyes, bathing, physical exercise, washing clothes and other daily activities can be exploited for teaching as well as the inculcation of good habits."

Means of Education

The scheme of basic education clarifies the means of education according to M.K. Gandhi. The most important means of education in basic scheme was craft. About this means of education Gandhi said, "The principal idea is to impart the whole education of body and the mind and the soul through the handicraft that is taught to the children. You have to draw out all that is in the child through teaching all the processes of the handicraft, and all your lessons in History, Geography, Arithmetic will be related to the craft." Thus, some handicraft was necessary to be the centre of the child's education. Besides, other crafts recommended were: weaving, carpentry, agriculture, gardening and other handicrafts and rural crafts. It was pointed out that the following criteria should be followed in deciding about the basic craft:

1. Craft fulfilling individual and social means.
2. Craft based upon local requirements.
3. Craft in tune with the local conditions.
4. Craft favourable to the interest, aptitude and ability of the child.
5. Less expensive and simple craft.
6. Craft leading to all round development of personality.

At the back of craft as the means of education were the psychological principles of education through activity as visible in the western play ways of education, project methods, etc. Besides, this means of education was economically useful as the basic craft could be utilised by the educand to earn his livelihood. It was also supported to create a tendency for physical labour in the educands. According to Gandhi, "Labour is the source of all wealth. All higher castes live on the exploitation of the lower castes. Wealth is inevitably reduced and large scale poverty occasioned." Thus, craft was a means to inculcate the lesson of physical and labour.

Another important element in the means of education in basic scheme was synthesis between the actual problems and life of education, between different subjects of the curriculum and finally between theoretical education and practical ability.

In order to implement the principle of synthesis in basic education it was insisted that the teachers and educands should" together formulate yearly projects divided into quarterly, monthly, weekly and daily projects. After this planning, the means such as raw material and necessary tools should be gathered. Efforts should be made to fulfil the schedule of the projects. Each project must be evaluated monthly or quarterly as the case may be. In the end the teachers should note their experiences in order to profit by them in future.

Types of Education

Our discussion of the Gandhian scheme of education so far shows his emphasis upon primary education and the education of the child. He, however, equally devoted his thought to the adult education also known as social education. He realised that in order to bring about a *Sarvodaya* Society in India, the views of the adults should be changed. Therefore, he made adult education programme a vital element of his political movement. Thousands of volunteers were trained in adult education at Sabarmati and Sevagram *Ashrams*. They spread in thousands of villages and hundreds of urban centres to educate the adult males and females in night schools. The help of thousands of regular teachers in so many educational institutions was also utilised for this purpose.

An important characteristic of Gandhian philosophy is the aim of *Sarvodaya*. Therefore, he planned different types of education for the country. Besides basic education and social education he thought seriously over rural education and education of women. This will be discussed in our discussion of education for different sections of society.

Medium of Education

A staunch votary of mother tongue as the medium of education, Gandhi said, "I must cling to my mother tongue as to my mother's breast, in spite of its shortcomings. It alone can give me the life giving milk." He was vehemently against English as the medium of education in this country. He said, "To inflict English on children is to stunt their natural growth and perhaps to kill originality in them." He pointed out to many modern western countries including U.S.S.R. who have made tremendous scientific progress without any help of English language. He maintained that our insistent on English is a remnant of our long slavery to the British. He was never prepared to accept this submission to foreign yoke. He maintained that the national language alone can be the vehicle of creating a common culture and rich literature. He was very much conversant with the language problem in India. He wanted to keep the country united particularly from the point of view of language. Therefore, he devised a common national language Hindustani which may be written in both Devanagari and Persian scripts. According to him there is no difference in Hindi and Urdu. While Hindi is Hindustani written in Devanagari script, Urdu is Hindustani written in Arabic script. Gandhi was in favour of mass language. Therefore, he opposed the inclusion of different terms from Sanskrit or Persian in Hindustani. His idea of making Hindustani the national language was rooted in the idea of Hindu-Muslim unity. He admitted that the Devanagari script should be used throughout the country but he also gave concession to Arabic script. It must be admitted here that his views on the language problem and the medium of education were coloured by his political ideas, if not prejudices. He also supported growth of regional languages in the country.

Teaching Methods

The teaching methods in the Gandhian scheme of education can be deduced from his basic education. As has been pointed out, Gandhi pleaded that the child should be educated through a basic craft. He should first be taught a basic craft from among the different types of it and other subjects such as Arithmetic, Language, Geography, History and Civics should be taught in association with the basic craft. In his educational institutions children were busy in craft activities for hours. There was no provision of rigid time table or ringing of the bell after every hour. There was no compulsion to work in the class room. The child was left free to select a craft according to his natural interest, abilities and the local conditions. He was also left free to work and develop his abilities according to his leanings. This method of teaching has been justified by western educationists. Rousseau insisted upon the value of total freedom in teaching methods. Herbert admitted the value of synthesis in education.

As has been already pointed out, an important characteristic of the teaching method in Gandhian scheme was synthesis. Projects were drawn for the year, quarter, month, week and the day. They were carried on according to schedule and reviewed periodically. The teacher profited by this review. He gathered experience to make better projects and implement them more successfully. This method was natural, saved time was interesting, synthesised knowledge and action, helped in transfer of learning and led to the development of high moral character. It was based upon the educational principle of proceeding from gross to subtle. It required experienced and able teachers who could synthesise the educand and his environment and the different parts of the curriculum. They should be trained for this purpose.

This teaching method of Gandhi's scheme of education had its advantages as well as disadvantages. It was pointed out that it converted school into mini-factories and prolonged hours of engagement in crafts hardly left any leisure to the children for recreation and extra-curricular activities. Gandhi thought that the sale proceeds of the products of basic crafts in an educational institution will be sufficient to meet the salaries of the teachers. This, however, could never be realised. It was based on false expectations. However, nobody can doubt Gandhi's intensive insight into the teaching methods of the children and adults so much clear in his plans of basic education and adult education.

Education for Different Sections of Society

We have already pointed out Gandhian scheme for education of different sections of society according to age. He planned equally well for the education of children, as well as the adults. On the basis of sex society is divided into two broad sections, male and female. Gandhi planned for the education of both these sections. Regeneration of Indian women was a part of the political movement of M.K. Gandhi. Therefore, he had to speak and write about the education of women of India. In the basic scheme of education and in his plans of adult education Gandhi did not make any distinction on the basis of sex. He recommended same primary and adult education both for male and female. He was, however, not very much in favour of co-education. He allowed co-education up to the age of eight years and then after 16 years of age. He, however, pleaded for separate educational institution for boys and girls in adolescent age. The selection of co-educational or otherwise institution was finally left to the discretion of the parents. Gandhi maintained that family alone can create suitable tendencies for the success of co-education in educational institutions. He strongly supported all types of education both for male and female.

Society is again divided into progressive and backward sections both socially as well economically. As a champion of the uplift of backward classes in the country Gandhi devised elaborate plans for the education of scheduled tribes and scheduled castes in India. These plans were mainly based upon local circumstances. They aimed at the unity of the nation without distinction of caste, language, religion, region or community etc. Thus, Gandhi planned for education suitable for all the sections of society. This was a necessary corollary to his social ideal of *Sarvodaya*. His scheme of education not only aimed at character building but also social, political and economic uplift of all the sections of the society.

Critical Evaluation

In planning for adults and women, as for children, Gandhi tried to present a plan to fulfill their particular needs. His plan of education was everywhere need-based. While fulfilling the needs of different sections of society his plan of education aimed at national regeneration. It was again guided by a more universal aim *Sarvodaya*, which means welfare not only in national but also in international affairs. Thus Gandhi's philosophy of education is based upon his humanism. He worshipped man in God. To him the sole aim of life was the worship of God, and the means of his worship was service of humanity. His own political, social and other activities had this aim in view. He said, "My duty is service of God and, therefore, service of humanity."[19] He did not confine his idea of humanity within national bounds, but sought to spread his message of non-violence throughout the world. His humanism was a direct corollary of his faith in *Vedanta* philosophy. He said, "I believe in the absolute oneness of God and, therefore, also of humanity. What though we have many bodies? We have but one soul. The rays of the sun are many through refraction. But they have the same source."[20] Though a staunch Hindu, Gandhi as a humanist, believed in equality of all religions and pleaded for the development of the sense of world religion among the new generation. He said, "I believe Hinduism to be a religion of truth but Islam and Christianity also are religions of truth. From your standpoint Christianity is true; Hinduism from my point."[21] Gandhi's so much emphasis upon truth and non-violence was also based upon his humanism. He realised that unless non-violence is made the law of our species human race cannot survive. Therefore, he pleaded for non-violence in every field of life. His philosophy of education can be called education for non-violence.

Humanism of Gandhi, however, was not of naturalistic or rational variety. On the other hand, his was the integral humanism derived from the humanistic tradition in *Gita,* He was not a rationalist. For him conscience was higher than reason. God is known through direct experience, through love and feeling, not through logic or reasoning. He believed in man's inner harmony with Nature and God. The trinity is in fact three aspects of the same unity. Similarly, in man also the physical, mental and other aspects are integrally related. Thus, Gandhi's philosophy of education was based upon harmony within man and harmony of man with other human beings and the Nature. This is also the result of non-violent attitude towards life. Non-violence, according to Gandhi, is not merely relative, it is not abstinence from all injury. It has also a positive aspect which in fact is more important. Thus, non-violence is love for all human beings, and it involves earnest efforts for the good of all. Thus ultimately, the ideal of *Sarvodaya* is a modern version of the ancient Indian integral humanism. This ideal of *Sarvodaya* as we have already pointed out, is the foundation of Gandhi's philosophy of education. Thus, Gandhi's philosophy of education is an attempt to build up an educational system on the philosophical basis of integral humanism.

As we have already pointed out at several places Gandhi's high optimism in basic education did not succeed. However, it laid down firmly the bases of free and compulsory education in this country. His schemes of adult education, women's education and education of backward classes were not followed in all their details. However, they undoubtedly laid down the direction in which education in this country should proceed. His Hindustani did not become national language. This honoured place was rightly given to Hindi in free India. But the idea of national integration at the basis of Gandhi's idea of national language has not been challenged by anyone. Broadly, the present day primary and adult social education in modern India follows the aims and ideals laid down by M. K. Gandhi.

References

1. Gandhi, M.K., *Harijan*, 31-7-37.
2. *Ibid.*, 11-9-37.
3. *Ibid.*
4. *Ibid.*, 27-5-39.
5. Gandhi, M.K., *Young India*, 14-11-29.

6. Gandhi, M.K., *Harijan,* 11-9-37.
7. *Ibid.,* 18-9-37.
8. *Reporting the Kothari Commission,* 1964-66.
9. Gandhi, M.K., *Harijan,* 26-3-31.
10. Gandhi, M.K., *To the Students,* (Ahmedabad: Navjivan Publishing House, 1949), p. 107.
11. Gandhi, M.K., *The Evolution of Educational Theory,* p. 146.
12. Gandhi, M.K., *Harijan,* Oct. 9, 1937, p. 293.
13. Gandhi, M.K., *Young India,* Aug. 11, 1928.
14. *Ibid.*
15. *Ibid., Oct.* 11, 1928.
16. Gandhi, M.K., *Harijan,* 9-3-47.
17. Gandhi, M.K., *Educational Reconstruction,* p. 66,
18. Patel, M.S., *The Educational Philosophy of Mahatma Gandhi,* (Ahmedabad: Navjivan Publishing House, 1952), p. 98-99.
19. Gandhi, M.K., *Harijan,* Oct. 9, 1937, p. 293.
20. Gandhi, M.K., *Young India,* 25-9-24.
21. Shukla, C.S., *Conversation of Gandhiji,* p. 30.

7

Rabindra Nath Tagore's Philosophy of Education

Among the contemporary Indian philosophers of education Rabindra Nath Tagore is one who may be called a humanist in the strict sense of the term. In the tradition of Indian humanism, his humanism, however, is not naturalistic but integral. His philosophy is cosmopolitan humanism and his theory of education is directly deduced from this philosophy.

The Concept of Universal Man

Philosophy of education cannot be understood without understanding the metaphysical theory. In the metaphysical theory of Rabindra Nath the most important idea is the concept of Universal Man. This is not a concept in the strict sense of the term, it is rather a poet's vision. Referring to Universal Man as the ultimate reality Rabindra Nath said, "Truth is the infinite pursued by science, while reality is the definition of the infinite which relates truth to the person. Reality is human; it is what we are conscious of, by which we are affected, that which we express."[1] This Universal Man is known by the individual not through his reason or logic but through direct realisation. In the words of Rabindra Nath, "Reality, in all its manifestations, reveals itself in the emotional and imaginative background of our mind. We know it, not because we think of it, but because we directly feel it. It is not banished from our conscious mind."[2] Thus Rabindra Nath cannot be called a rationalist as the naturalistic humanist is known to be. In the Indian tradition he considered man more than reason, a soul, a spirit, a finite-infinite being. The concept of Universal Man in his philosophy agrees with the cosmic vision of Divine in *Gita*. The Universal Man is at the back of all movements, all change, all order and system in the universe. Man is very much a part of Him. Man and Nature cannot be conceived separate from God. The Universal Man includes both. As Rabindra Nath himself admitted, "I have never looked at God, Man and Nature as problems which can be considered in isolation from each other. I could never conceive of their occupying watertight compartments."[3]

This Universal Man is in every individual person. He lives even in the humblest man. Therefore, even the most poor, illiterate and humble human being should not be neglected by us. The worship of the poor is a direct corollary of Rabindra Nath's vision of the Universal Man. As he said, "He is there where the tiller is tilling the hard ground and where the path maker is breaking stones. He is with them in sun and in shower, and His garment is covered with dust. Put off thy holy mantle and even like Him come down on the dusty soil."[4]

Here a metaphysical problem arises in assigning personality to the ultimate reality. How can a person be the ultimate reality since personality is limited and distinct? It may be remembered in this connection that for Rabindra Nath personality is not something limited and mundane but also unlimited and supra-mundane, while in the human being it is found in the first form, in Universal Man it may be seen in the second meaning. Explaining this meaning of the Universal Man, Rabindra Nath said, "This personality which is the conscious principle of oneness, the centre of relationships, is the reality,—therefore the ultimate object of attainment. I must emphasize this fact, that this world is a real world only in its relation to a central personality. When that centre is taken away, then it falls to pieces, become a heap of abstractions, matter and force, logical symbols and even those,—the thinnest semblances of reality—would vanish into absolute nothingness, if the logical person in the centre, to whom they are related in some harmony of reason, were nowhere."[5] God is the perfect person. Human beings are persons in an imperfect sense. While man is an individual god,

God is Universal Man. He is the supreme person. This supreme person has been seen in two forms, *Saguna* and *Nirguna*. Both are two aspects of the same Universal Man. God is the perfect ideal type of man. He possesses all human qualities. In the words of Rabindra Nath,. "All human qualities find their suggestion in God."[6] He has even the trait of action which is characteristically human. In the words of Rabindra Nath, "Action must be attributed to Him, otherwise how could he give himself."[7] He is the meeting ground of man and the world. It is in Him alone that human beings exchange their experiences. According to Rabindra Nath, "The relational world is for me both individual and universal. My world is mine, but it is also yours. . . . It is not in my own individual personality that Reality is contained, but in an Infinite personality."[8]

Aims of Education

According to Rabindra Nath, the aim of education is self-realisation. He is a poet and a saint who through his imagination and insight, realised the universal soul within himself and in Nature. According to him this realisation by every one is the goal of education. Self-realisation, according to Rabindra Nath, means the realisation of the universal soul is one's self. Man's aim in life is to achieve this status. It is a process which cannot be realised without education. In the absence of education the individual will be deprived of self-realisation. Rabindra Nath does not find any dichotomy between thought and life, philosophy and education. He believes that everyone is potentially divine and everyone can realise this potentiality. His philosophy is very much influenced by the *Gita* and the *Upanisads*. He is, however, well aware of the educational ideas prevalent in the West. Therefore, like Vivekananda, he synthesizes the ancient Vedantic traditions with the modern Western scientific attitude in formulating the goal of education.

Integral Development

Defining the aims of education, Rabindra Nath says, "The fundamental purpose of education is not merely to enrich ourselves through the fullness of knowledge, but also to establish the bond of love and friendship between man and man."[9] This is the humanistic aim of education in Tagore's philosophy. His approach to ultimate reality is integral. He believes in an inner harmony between man and Nature and God. The trinity, man, Nature and God are in fact three aspects of the same reality. In man, again, the physical, the mental and the spiritual aspects are equally important and internally related. Therefore, like Sri Aurobindo, Rabindra Nath believes in a multi-sided education with physical, intellectual, moral and religious aims.

Physical Development

Like Vivekananda, Rebindranath condemned the prevalent system of education which partially exercised the intellect only to the entire neglect of the body. According to Rabindra Nath, education of the body in the real sense, "does not exist in play and exercise but in applying the body systematically to some useful work."[10] Thus, one of the aims of education according to Rabindra Nath, is physical development. It is hence that he so much emphasizes games in school education. Pointing out the value of physical activities in the child's education he says, "Even if they learnt nothing, they would have had ample time for play, climbing trees, diving into ponds, plucking and tearing flowers, perpetrating thousand and one mischief on Mother Nature, they would have obtained the nourishment of the body, happiness of mind and the satisfaction of the natural impulses of childhood."[11] Thus physical fitness is the first cardinal principle in the child's development. This is realised through his intimate contact with Nature. As a poet Tagore very well realises the life giving value of Nature's contact with man. About the child's contact with the Nature he says, "I speak in very moderate terms: Seven years—till then let the child have nothing to do with clothes and shame. Till then let Nature alone conduct the indispensable education of the savage."[12] This is particularly important for the educational institutions in our society. Almost all contemporary Indian philosophers of education, including Gandhi, Vivekananda, Dayananda and Sri Aurobindo, besides Tagore, lay emphasis upon the importance of setting educational institutions in natural environment, so that the educands may learn by their touch with Nature.

Mental Development

Besides the physical aim of education, Tagore equally lays emphasis upon the mental aim of education. Like Vivekananda he is critical of the prevalent system of education which laid sole emphasis upon bookish learning. Presenting this attitude, he says, "We touch the world not with our mind, but with our books."[13] This is deplorable. Intellectualism takes us away from Nature and creates a gulf between man and man. To quote Rabindra Nath, "We know the people of books, not those of the world; the former are interesting to us but the latter tiresome."[14] In fact, the intellectual aim of education, according to Rabindra Nath, is the development of the intellectual faculties such as logical thinking, critical appraisal and assimilation. Two mental faculties which should be developed through education are: the power of thinking and the power of imagination. Both these are necessary for real manhood. Rabindra Nath criticises the prevalent system of education which puts too much stress on memory and too little on imagination and thinking. He suggests, "Ever since childhood, instead of putting all the burden on the memory, the power of thinking and the power of imagination should also be given opportunities for free exercise."[15]

Harmony with Environment

In the end, the aim of education according to Rabindra Nath is the harmony of the educand with the environment. The educand should know his environment and create harmony with it. To quote Rabindra Nath, "True education consists in knowing the use of any useful material that has been collected, to know its real nature and to build along with life a real shelter for life."[16] This is particularly true about the rural education. Education should facilitate the educand's assimilation of his national culture. Through education, the educand should imbibe his cultural heritage and should be able to use it in his inter-action with the environment. Explaining this aim of education, Rabindra Nath says, "If we believe that the chief aim of education for an Indian, is to be initiated into this unique pursuit of India, then we must constantly remember that neither the education of the senses, nor the education of the intellect, but the education of the feeling should receive the place of honour in our schools

. . . Our true education is possible only in the forest, through intimate contact with Nature and purifying austere pursuits."[17]

Earning Livelihood

Thus, about the aim of education, Tagore's approach is realistic. He, however, does not favour the utilitarian aim of education. This is his objection against the imposition of British system of education upon India. He says, "Knowledge has two departments: one pure knowledge, the other utilitarian knowledge. Whatever is worth knowing is knowledge. It should be known equally by man and women, not for practical utility, but for the sake of knowing . . . The desire to know is the law of human nature."[18] But Rabindra Nath does not ignore the earning of livelihood aim of education. He appreciates the practical bias in Western system of education. Though he does not want to make education an instrument for earning bread alone but he admits that bread earning is a necessary part of any sound goal of education. Therefore, he says, "From the very beginning, such education should be imparted to them (village folks) that they may know well what mass welfare means and may become practically efficient in all respects for earning their livelihood."[19] While he is critical of the British system of education which wanted to create clerks out of the Indian educated people, he emphasises that the real aim of education is to develop men and women who may be able to fulfill the needs of the country. In his own words, "One of the main aims of education is to prepare the individual for the service of the country."[20]

Multi-sided Aim

The above discussion concerning the means of education according to Rabindra Nath, makes it clear that his is a multisided attack on this problem. He is against any one sided aim of education. He is a humanist. A humanistic aim of education requires a multi-sided approach.

Education at Shantiniketan

Educational Trinity

Explaining educational trinity in the educational philosophy of Rabindra Nath, S.S. Sinha writes, "Santiniketan. Visva-Bharati and Sriniketan may be said to constitute Tagore's educational trinity through which he endeavoured to develop his educational theme in three different complementary directions. The school came first in the field and was far away the most important, as it embodied all the poet's main teachings about education. The three institutions thus displayed a discernible pattern of growth and expansion, illustrating their underlying creative unity."[21]

Ideal of Shantiniketan

The most important in this trinity is the Shantiniketan. Explaining his idea of Santiniketan to Sri J.C. Bose, Rabindra Nath wrote, "I am trying to start a school at Santiniketan. It will be conducted just on the lines of residential institutions of ancient times. There shall not be the least trace of luxury. We shall not be able to become true Hindus if all of us, whether rich or poor, do not learn rigid *Brahmacarya*: Frivolity and luxury are degenerating us. Wants of all descriptions are ever-powering us only because we are failing to accept poverty with equanimity."[22] Santiniketan was started on a small scale with a school and a boarding house. The school was named '*Brahmacaryasram*' and inaugurated on 22nd of December, 1901. The most important consideration in the school was the provision of a suitable environment for the ail round development of the educands. In brief, it was the students' own world in which they themselves managed everything and developed through this experiment. Clarifying this pattern Rabindra Nath says, "I always try to impress upon their minds that is their own world, upon which their life ought fully and freely to react. In the school administration they have their place, and in the matter of punishment we mostly rely upon their own court of justice."[23]

Due to his wide travels in Asia and Europe Tagore was convinced that human good lies in the emergence of the world society, and the communication among various human beings. He wanted to build up an educational institution for the meeting of East and West. Such a place was developed in the form of Visva-Bharati at Santiniketan. Explaining the aim and function of Visva-Bharati Rabindra Nath said, "Being strongly impressed with the need and the responsibility, which every individual must today realize according to his power, I have formed the nucleus of an International University in India, as one of best means of promoting mutual understanding between the East and the West. This institution, according to the plan I have in mind, invites students from the West and the East to study the different systems of Indian philosophy, literature, art and music in their proper environment encouraging them to carry on research work in collaboration with the scholars already engaged in the task."[24] Thus Visva-Bharati was developed as a centre of Indian culture, Eastern culture, international culture and mass welfare and rural reconstruction. This ideal is being realised through the efforts of both the teachers and the students.

Principles of Education

Through his education trinity Rabindra Nath aims to develop an ideal educational system in India. His aim of education is one of the most comprehensive, including various aspects of human personality and different strata of Indian society and the world community. He lays emphasis on physical, mental, moral, religious, spiritual, in fact all the aspects of a man's education. Thus he developed his plan on a very comprehensive perspective. His educational plan is activity-oriented. Its aim is to develop an all round human personality. Its means include extra-curricular activities besides bookish education. The curriculum in his educational institution is not fixed but changes according to the needs of the educands. His only emphasis is on life, life of the individual, of the rural masses, of the poor Indians and that of man as a member of an International community. He wants to make students self-reliant. His aim is to develop a sort of communion between man and Nature.

Freedom is the key-note of Rabindra Nath's system of education. He believes in complete freedom of all types, freedom of intellectual decision, knowledge, action and worship. This freedom can be achieved by the practice of equanimity, harmony and balance. Through this practice the educand may learn to distinguish between truth and false, natural and artificial, relevant and irrelevant, permanent and temporary, liberal and narrow, universal and individual. Thus the educand may achieve a harmony in the true, natural, relevant, permanent and real elements. Once he acquires this ability he may progress by self-guidance. This in fact is the real meaning of self-education based on self-realisation.

Education, according to Rabindra Nath, is a progress of self-realisation. This self-realisation lies in the attainment of freedom when intelligence, feeling and determination work freely. It is not the absence of control but self-control. Once it is achieved there is no danger of straying from the right path because the senses, intelligence, emotions, feelings and mental powers of the educated person are guided by his own-self.

The ideal educational system, according to Rabindra Nath, should aim at man's perfection. Perfection means the development of all the aspects of human personality. This is the sole aim of education. This again, should be realised on a universal scale since unless the individual acquires an abiding faith in the universal soul he cannot realise itself. Thus, education should lead to the realization of universal man.

As is clear by the above discussion, Rabindra Nath tries to utilise the findings of modern Western educational psychology as well as the ancient wisdom of India. In his ideal educational system, the educational process is mainly functional with activity as its basis. It requires both the educand and the educator to be always active. In it learning and practice go together. Rabindra Nath is against all types of orthodox discipline and corporal punishment. He believes that discipline through rod is not at all necessary in educational institutions. It only leads to depression. On the other hand, Rabindra Nath observes, "I have a deep-rooted conviction that only through freedom can man attain his fullness of growth."[25] In his ideal educational system, therefore, all discipline is self-discipline. The educands are allowed to commit mistakes and learn through them. Like Sri Aurobindo International University. Shantiniketan has a type of self-government.

Rabindra Nath was against the then prevalent system of educands evaluation. In this field also he recommends the principle of self-determination. He suggests that invigilation is absolutely unnecessary and the examinees may themselves take their question papers and answer them.

The Siksa-Satra Experiment

The Siksa-Satra Experiment of Sriniketan embodies Tagore's idea of a rural institute. Being based upon the needs of rural people, it was different from Santiniketan, Rabindra Nath had personal experience of the difficulties of rural people and he was very much convinced of the need of education among them. He realised that a universal education is very much necessary for the regeneration of the Indian villages. Therefore, he started the *Siksa Satra* experiment at Sriniketan. This experiment was based on the faith that, "Given the right tools and organisations, the villagers can help themselves upward by development based on research and by a welfare programme based upon the study of human need in every village in India."[26]

Siksa Satra experiment was started to fulfil the needs of education in rural setting particularly. Its activities, therefore, not only included literacy but also social reform. It sought to realise the ideal of rural welfare. It endeavoured to remove the social evil from the village society. In the economic field, it tried to teach the villagers the methods and techniques of farming and other vocations. In brief, its aim was to realise an all round rural reconstruction.

The most important means of education, according to Rabindra Nath is the environment of the child. The importance of natural environment has been accepted by almost all contemporary educational psychologists. It is through the natural environment that the child trains his senses by his contact with plants and trees, flowers and leaves. Education, according to Rabindra Nath, should be imparted "in an institution where the first great lesson in the perfect union of man and Nature, not only through love but through active communication, can be had unobstructed."[27] It is only in a natural environment that the child can realise the presence of a universal soul which is the root of his existence and also that of Nature. Like Sri Aurobindo, Rabindra Nath maintains that the teaching of different subjects may be made natural through the intelligent utilisation of the child's environment. The child's knowledge of science may be helped by his observation of insects and animals, plants and trees, stars and moon and sun. His emotional and aesthetic training is helped by his observation and appreciation of forms and colours and movement in Nature. The natural environment richly contributes to the development of the child's sense organs and mind. His creative powers are expressed through his contact with natural objects. His extra-curricular activities in a natural environment results in the development of different virtues.

Rabindra Nath regrets that, "Ours is the only country in recent history where the educational institutions stopped at their boundary walls and were dissociated from the wide world outside."[28] Pointing out to the gulf between bookish knowledge and the child's environment Tagore laments, that the current education does not help in making the educand either an efficient worker or a good citizen. Both these are equally necessary. To quote Rabindra Nath, "It is not enough for a farmer boy only to grow into a good farmer, but he should also grow into a good citizen of the country."[29]

Besides natural environment, social environment is no less important in the development of the child, in fact it is more valuable. The social environment makes the surroundings of the children in which they fulfil their needs and drives and develop their beliefs and ideas. It is the knowledge of this environment which creates in the child the sense of essential unity of mankind. The impact of the social environment is more explicit in the relationship between the educator and the educand on the one hand and the educand and his companions on the other. If this relationship is based upon love, sympathy and mutual understanding the educand easily develops moral virtues. According to Rabindra Nath, every educated person should learn to play a role in the human society according to his particular traits. The cultural environment again is a part of the social environment. In educational institutions this is created through extra-curricular activities and cultural programmes.

The most important means of education is the medium of instruction. Almost all contemporary Indian philosophers of education pleaded for the adoption of mother tongue as the medium of child's education. And Tagore is no exception to this rule. He said, "If education does not enter into the deeper strata of the society and does not attain permanence through mingling with the living stream of the mother-tongue, then, however, much it may bubble up and dance like foam on the surface, it can only become an object of temporary beauty but can never become a lasting foundation of life."[30] India needs education on a large scale particularly technical and vocational education.

Tagore realised that this is possible only through the mother-tongue. The use of English language for this purpose had been the main cause of the poor state of education in India. Unless our educational institutions adopt regional languages and national language as medium of instruction and unless sufficient books are available in these languages, the aim of universal education in India cannot be realised.

Rabindra Nath is very much in favour of reviving the old rural institutions in the villages. He attached much educational value to community entertainment, recitals of *Ramayana* and *Mahabharata* and religious *Kirtans*. These are very much useful in moral and religious education. Besides, the community fairs organised in villages from time-to-time are also useful means of education. The vocational education in the villages is very much helped by the fairs. To make education mass-oriented the means of education should also be indigenous and easily available in the rural areas.

Critical Evaluation

Thus, Rabindra Nath's philosophy of education aims at developing a system of education for human re-generation. Man is in the centre of all his thinking, his philosophy, religion, literature, poetry, social activities and educational programmes. He is a humanist in the real sense of the term, not a naturalistic humanist but an integral humanist in the Indian tradition. He is not a rationalist but believes in something higher than reason in man. He does not think science alone to be capable of delivering the human goods but wants to synthesize it with *Vedanta*. He is a nationalist and at the same time an internationalist. To him the ultimate God is the universal man and the only aim of all the man's activities was the realisation of this God. Human re-generation is his sole aim and only ideal. His educational system is a means to achieve this aim. He, therefore, bases his educational system on essential human virtues such as freedom, purity, sympathy, perfection and world brotherhood.

Like other contemporary Indian thinkers of his time Tagore objected to the prevalent system of education due to its origination in a foreign country. He protested against emphasis on foreign language resulting in the alienation of the educated people from the general society. He tried to build up educational centres where these defects may be removed. He deliberated on different problems of Indian society particularly that of the rural people and tried to remove them through education. His educational system was a synthesis of East and West, ancient and modern, science and vedanta. It is hence that man like Jawaharlal Nehru considered Visva-Bharati as the true representative of India.

Pointing out humanist element in Tagore's philosophy Humayun Kabir wrote, "Rabindra Nath Tagore was one of the greatest humanists that the world has known. The keynote of his life was resistance to tyranny in all forms. He struggled against economic exploitation, political subjugation, social inertia and injustice and religious intolerance and insensitiveness."[31] The humanism of Rabindra Nath is generally expressed to his literature. Besides literature Tagore's humanism is expressed by his idea of Religion of Man. In his works everywhere he laid emphasis upon the uniqueness of the human individual, his greatness in the world of living beings and his intimate relationship with Nature and God. It is this humanism which made Rabindra Nath work relentlessly for the establishment of a cosmopolitan educational institution in the form of Santiniketan. His educational philosophy is no less an example of his humanism than his literature and religious writings. He tried to build up an ideal educational system and experimented in all its branches such as aims, medium, means, curriculum, administration and extra-curricular activities. One may not agree with the details of his educational system and may not accept all of it but none can deny that it was a bold attempt based upon a very comprehensive philosophy and with the most human intention of developing perfect men and women, citizens of a world community.

References

1. Neogi, p. (Ed), *Rabindra Nath Tagore on Art and Aesthetics*, p. 76.
2. Tagore, R.N., *The Religion of Man* (London: George Allen & Unwin, 1932), p. 130.
3. Tagore, R.N., '*Amar Dharma*'.

4. Tagore, R.N., *Gitanjali,* Song 11 (London: Macmillan & Co., 1962).
5. Tagore, R.N., *Personality* (London: Macmillan & Co., 1954), p. 98.
6. *Man,* p. 28.
7. 'Karmoyoga' *Santiniketan,* XIII Series.
8. Tagore, R.N., *Personality,* p. 58.
9. *Bhartiya Visva Vidyalya Adrasa, 'Siksa,'* (1342), B.S.Ed., p. 270.
10. Tagore, R.N., *'Alochana',* July, 1925.
11. *'Siksa'* (1342), B.S.Ed., p. 2
12. Ibid., p. 84.
13. *Ibid.,* p. 90.
14. *Ibid.,* p. 91.
15. *'Siksar Herpher',* p. 8.
16. *Ibid.*
17. *'Siksa'* (1342, B.S.), p. 145.
18. *'Siksa',* 1351 Ed., Vol. I, p. 151.
19. 'Swadhin Siksa' p, 522.
20. *Rabindra Rachanavali,* Vol. XII, p. 517.
21. Sinha, S.S., *Social Thinking of Rabindra Nath Tagore* (Bombay; Asia Publishing House, 1962), p. 54.
22. *Sabuj Patra,* Vol. II (Sravan 9, 1308 B.S.), p. 30.
23. Tagore, R.N., *Personality,* p. 146.
24. Tagore, R.N., *An Eastern University,* p. 2.
25. Tagore, R.N., The School Master *Modern Review,* October 1924.
26. Elmhirst, L., 'Sriniketan' *Visva-Bharati Quarterly,* (1955), p. 4.
27. Tagore, R.N., 'A Poet's School', *Visva-Bharati Bulletin,* No. 9. (1928), p.8.
28. 'Siksar Vikiran', *Siksa,* 1442 B.S.Ed., p. 236.
29. *Rabindra Nath Rachanavali,* Vol. XII, p. 516.
30. *Ibid.,* p. 618.
31. Bhattacharya, K., 'Rabindra Nath on Religion', *Homage from Visva-Bharati* (Santiniketan, 1962), p. 32.

8

S. Radhakrishnan's Philosophy of Education

Among the contemporary Indian philosophers of education Dr. Sarvapalli Radhakrishnan was the only thinker who had long experience of the field of education as a professor in Eastern and Western universities and also as a Vice-Chancellor. As the head of the University Education Commission he had an occasion to probe deep into the problems of higher education in India. Along with his wide experience of the field of education, Radhakrishnan had wide learning and deep insight into Indian and Western philosophy, ancient and contemporary. Therefore, he was undoubtedly one of the most qualified persons to speak about Indian philosophy of education with authority. His views are found scattered in his various books such as *An Idealist View of Life, The Philosophy of Rabindra Nath Tagore, The Brahmasutra, The Bhagvadgita, The Hindu View of Life, Eastern Religion and Western Thought*, etc. Besides his speeches are an important source of his philosophy of education.

Analysis of Human Nature

Radhakrishnan was an idealist philosopher. He was an advocate of ancient Indian *Vedanta* philosophy. This is very much clear from his works, *The Hindu View of Life, Brahmasutra, An Idealist View of Life*, etc. He defined philosophy as a combination of reflection and intuition.[1] According to him the aim of philosophy is to search that synthesis which may include all the aspects of creation. Philosophy, according to him, "is an attempt of human being to know the problems of creation and the nature of ultimate reality."[2] In epistemology Radhakrishnan admitted the value of both reason and faith, logic and experience. He admitted the value of perceptual, conceptual and intuitive knowledge in education. According to him intuitive knowledge is the highest knowledge.[3] It is an integral experience. He admitted mystic experience as a part of intuitive experience.[4] Total experience is gained by total self and it is much higher than any other experience gained by any part of man's being.[5] Creative insight has an important place in total knowledge. Radhakrishnan, however, is nowhere an anti-intellectualist like Bergson or Bradley. He was not a mystic in the final analysis. His philosophy has been rightly interpreted as Integral experience.[6] Integral experience finds place for every other type of experience in it.

Human personality, according to Radhakrishnan, is not determined by physical environment, economic or otherwise. So far as physical changes are concerned they may be generally determined by the environment but the human will is free to decide to win or lose. The real human freedom is the freedom of will. This has been granted to man. In the tradition of ancient Indian thinkers Radhakrishnan had admitted the principle of *Karma*. According to this principle our present is determined by our past and the future depends upon the present. In the words of Radhakrishnan, "*Karma* or relationships with the past does not mean that man cannot do anything freely but free action is involved in it."[7] The law of *Karma* is not fatalism. According to it, "An individual will gain according to the use of his energy. The world will respond to the individual *Jivatma's* demand. The Nature will reply the insistent call of the man."[8] Thus, like Karl Marx, Radhakrishnan believed that man can change the world. On the basis of his will he can make his future. The principles of Nature are the principles of justice. In Nature and in human world, everywhere one universal divine law functions. Therefore, the law of *Karma* is not an external but an internal determinant of human life.

In the line of evolution, man is distinguished by self-consciousness which is not found either in plants or in animals.

Therefore, the mental processes cannot be interpreted in terms of physical changes. The physical movements do not explain total behaviour. Modern psychology takes a one-sided view of man while presenting behaviouristic interpretation. Behaviourism has only historical value. Man's behaviour cannot be explained by stimulus-response formula. An organism is not merely a sum total of parts. Its parts are internally related. Consciousness does not come out of matter, it is a new creation. Again, self-consciousness is not a biological product. Therefore, psychological phenomena should not be explained in physiological or biological terms. With the evolution of self-consciousness Nature evolves to a new level of existence. The self-conscious man is rational. Self-realisation is the aim of life. This self is the Spirit. In the words of Radhakrishnan, "Spirit is life, not thing, power not status, real in itself and through itself and cannot be compared to any substance subjective or objective."[9] The spirit expresses as itself, God and the world. Thus human nature is essentially spiritual. Spiritual also means natural because nature is as much an expression of spirit as the self. Human life is not only natural but also divine since its essential nature is Spirit. The world is a gradual evolution towards Spirit. In this evolution man is at the apex. This evolution is both emergent as well as continuous. What is not cannot happen, whatever is it develops. This metaphysical hypothesis is very important in the philosophy of education. The child will develop only that which is potential in it. What is not implicit cannot be explicit. However, every level of evolution expresses new elements. The characteristics of Spirit are seen in creativity, change, system and progress. There are the characteristics of every field of life and so of education. Education aims at complete expression of the inherent Spirit in man.

It appears that Radhakrishnan's philosophy is mysticism so far as the concept of Spirit is concerned. In his book *An Idealist View of Life*, Radhakrishnan has called Spirit total *Brahman.*[10] *Brahman* precedes creation. Identifying God and creator Radhakrishnan said, "They are the different forms of seeing the same ultimate reality."[11] Thus, like Sri Aurobindo Radhakrishnan believes the world to be the expression of God. This metaphysical proposition lays down the spiritual goal of education and certifies its possibility. In fact, Radhakrishnan has synthesised idealism, and realism mysticism and pragmatism in his philosophy of education. He welcomes all sorts of experience to arrive at some general principles. As he said, "We should weave different parts of experience in a total pattern. We should keep our general ideas connected so that different experiences may be explained."[12]

In spite of being a votary of science Radhakrishnan is not a determinist or environmentalist. This fact is of capital importance in his explanation of human nature and in his philosophy of education. Science proves that every effect has a cause but it does not definitely prove the cause of every effect. As David Hume has rightly pointed out, the principle of causation in the field of science is a mere probability. So far as physical incidents are concerned, they are determined by natural laws but man has been provided freedom of choice in life. He is not free to choose his cards but he is free to play, win or lose as he likes. This freedom of winning or losing is given to man. This victory or defeat is not of physical happenings but of the mind. The real freedom is the freedom of the will.

Criticism of Present System of Education

As the chairman of University Education Commission Radhakrishnan had an occasion to examine different aspects of Indian education in details. The terms of reference of this commission of enquiry were as follows:

(a) The aims and objects of university education and research in India.

(b) The changes considered necessary and desirable in the constitution, control, functions and jurisdiction of universities in India and their relations with Government, Central and Provincial.

(c) The finance of universities.

(d) The maintenance of the highest standards of teaching and examination in the universities and colleges under their control.

(e) The course of study in the universities with special reference to the maintenance of a sound balance between the Humanities and Sciences and between Pure Science and Technological Training and the duration of such courses.

(f) The standards of admission to university courses of study with reference to the desirability of an independent university entrance examination and the avoidance of unfair discrimination which militates against Fundamental Right 23(2).

(g) The medium of instruction in the universities.

(h) The provision for advanced study in Indian culture, history, literatures, languages, philosophy and fine arts.

(i) The need for more universities on a regional or other basis.

(j) The organisation of advanced research in all branches of knowledge in the universities and institutes of higher research in a well co-ordinated fashion avoiding waste of effort and resources.

(k) Religious instruction in the universities.

(l) The special problems of the Banaras Hindu University, the Aligarh Muslim University, the Delhi University and other institutions of an all-India character.

(m) The qualifications, conditions of service, salaries, privileges and functions of teachers and the encouragement of original research by teachers.

(n) The discipline of students, hostels and the organisation of tutorial work and any other matter which is germane to a complete and comprehensive enquiry into all aspects of university education and advanced research in India.

The commission pointed to the following grave defects in the present system of education:

1. In comparison to the universities in West the standard of people in Indian universities is very low. This is particularly due to the lower standard of education on intermediate stage.
2. The condition of teachers in Indian universities is far from being satisfactory. Their salary is inadequate and the working conditions are far from satisfactory. Therefore, able persons are not coming forward to take up the career of teaching.

3. The curriculum is not sufficiently diversified and integrated.
4. There are not sufficient vocational, engineering and technological institutions in the country.
5. National and regional languages have not been given sufficient opportunities to develop.
6. The examination system is far from being objective. It is full of grave defects.
7. The administration system does not find place for all the sections of society concerned with education.
8. The Government is not providing sufficient economic support to the institutions of higher education.
9. As the universities are functioning properly they are not fulfilling the important purpose of creating new generation of leaders in democracy.
10. Women education has not been extended sufficiently.
11. Rural education, necessary in a country like India, has been neglected.
12. Religious education has been generally sectarian which is not consistent in a secular State.

Aims of Education

Dr. Radhakrishnan recommended the following aims of education for higher education in India:

(i) To teach that life has a meaning.
(ii) To awaken the innate ability to live the life of soul by developing wisdom.
(iii) To acquaint with the social philosophy which should govern all our institutions—educational as well as economic and political.
(iv) To train for democracy.
(v) To train for self-development.
(vi) To develop certain values like fearlessness of mind, strength of conscience and integrity of purpose.
(vii) To acquaint with cultural heritage for its regeneration.
(viii) To enable to know that education is a life-long process.
(ix) To develop understanding of the present as well as of the past.
(x) To impart vocational and professional training.

Criticising the present system of education Radhakrishnan said, "Our education has not freed us from the intellectual bondage. It stimulates the mind without satisfying it."[13] Freedom, according to Radhakrishnan, is the goal of education. He lamented that the present system of education does not grow free thinking among students. The student does not know what is higher thinking. He does not develop any creativity. Our institutions are preparing human machines not developed human beings. The true education should aim at developing a total human personality, a free mind, a multisided growth, a creative aptitude and a spiritual evolution. The aim of life according to Radhakrishnan is to train the mind. As he said, "The real aim of education is to help man to know the inner essence."[14] Physical success and material progress is not the aim of education. True education does not aim at any diploma or degree. It is self-development. In the words of Radhakrishnan, "The real aim of education is this that the character of man may become rhythmic and his soul creative."[15] The primary aim of education from beginning to end is to attain knowledge. This knowledge, however, cannot be achieved only through books. The books cannot transform human personality. This transformation is the real aim of education. Transformation can be achieved only by putting knowledge in practice. Transformation is necessary for the realisation of human freedom. According to Radhakrishnan, "The freedom of human soul is the most valuable."[16] Therefore, education should aim at realisation of this freedom. This freedom again is the basis of character formation.

According to almost all contemporary Indian philosophers of education, education is a process of man-making. Man-making means character formation. As Radhakrishnan rightly pointed out, "The fate of a nation depends upon character. A country whose people have low character can never become great. When we want to build a great nation, we should educate more and more young men and women in such a way that they may have strength of character."[17] In a moral character, Radhakrishnan placed world fraternity as the highest virtue. His aim of education is humanist and internationalist.

Education aims at teaching self-expression. This is possible only through the mastery of language. In the end no education is complete without the development of intuition. The ancient Indian *Upanisads* identify intuition with wisdom and education. Intuition, however, cannot be achieved by the study of books alone. It requires guidance by the ability test. Therefore, Radhakrishnan insisted upon the appointment of able teachers particularly in the institutions of higher learning.

Means of Education

Radhakrishnan strongly favoured modern means of education. He laid down the standards of teaching at various levels of education in the report of commission headed by him. He maintained that students of different professions should be given practical training as far as possible. Elaborating this principle, the University Education Commission under him made the following recommendations:

(a) ***Agriculture***: The study of agriculture in primary, secondary and higher education be given high priority in national economic planning. So far as is feasible, agricultural education be given a rural setting.

(b) ***Commerce***: A commerce student should be given opportunities for practical work in three or four different kinds of firms.

(c) ***Education***: *The* course be remodelled and more time given to school practice and more weight to practice in assessing the student's performances.

(d) ***Engineering and Technology***: The number of engineering schools of different grades be increased particularly for training of grades 4 and 5 (foremen, craftsmen, draftsmen, overseers, etc.).

In establishing new engineering colleges or institutes there should be fresh, critical inquiry as to the types of engineering service needed in India. Uncritical repetition and imitation of existing institutions here and abroad should be avoided.

(e) ***Law***: A three-year degree course be offered in special legal subjects. Students pursuing degree course in law shall not be permitted to carry other degree courses simultaneously except in a few instances where advanced students have proved their interest and are studying related subjects in law and some other fields.

*(f) **Medicine***: The maximum number of admission to a medical college be 100, provided the staff and equipment for that number are available.

Types of Education

The means of education will be further clarified by a review of Radhakrishnan's views about various types of education. These are as follows:

1. ***Moral Education***: Like Vivekananda, Sri Aurobindo and M.K. Gandhi, Radhakrishnan wanted to make moral education a compulsory part of education at primary and secondary levels. Without it the educational institutions cannot fulfill their objective of educating the youth of the country. Moral character has been given the most important place in Indian culture. Moral education is the education of will. It starts in the family. In the school the educand learns moral norms in the imitation of the conduct of the teachers. The moral education clarifies the goal of life without which no meaningful life is possible. The greatness of a country cannot be measured by its progress in physical civilisation but by its moral and spiritual advancement. Therefore, whatever is done for the achievement of vocational goal, education cannot be complete without moral instruction. This has become even more important in the face of the fact that morality is the only reliable instrument for saving the world from the catastrophe of a future world war. The seeds of morality will be sown in educational institutions. Therefore, Radhakrishnan advised that society ought to be based on proper foundation. Economically prosperous man is not a perfect human being. A perfect being requires bliss and beauty of the soul which should be full of love and faith and endeavours for rejuvenating humanity.[18]

2. ***Religious Education***: Along with other contemporary Indian *Neo-Vedanta* philosophers of education, Radhakrishnan supports religious education. Religious education for him, however, is not the instruction of a particular religion. It is a means for developing spiritual intuition because, "The aim of religion is spiritual and not merely a change in metaphysical ideas."[19] Religious education is a means for propagation of the ideal of world brotherhood. According to Radhakrishnan, the

modern substitutes of religion such as communism cannot fulfill any useful purpose. Real religion is spiritual religion. Therefore religious education will provide freedom and spiritual progress to the educand. It is not contrary to the education of science but complimentary to it. India can progress in science in spite of its religious character. From this viewpoint Radhakrishnan is not prepared to accept secularism as meaning aversion to religion. According to him the only secularism worth the name means that every individual has full liberty to follow his religion. Radhakrishnan himself gives highest importance to *The Bhagvadgita* but does not derogate the importance of the scriptures of other religion. About *The Bhavadgita* he wrote, "*Bhagvadgita* has everything, rational, moral and spiritual, an answer to every question of human progress and its perfection."[20] Such a book may be the basis of religious education. However, religious education is in fact spiritual education. It is a means while spiritual education is the end. The University Education Commission, under the chairmanship of Radhakrishnan, made the following recommendations about religious education:

(a) All educational institutions should start work with a few minutes for silent meditation.

(b) In the first year lives of the great religious leaders like Gautama the Buddha, Confucius, Zoroaster, Socrates, Jesus, Samkara, Ramanuja, Madhva, Mohammad, Kabir, Nanak, Gandhi be taught.

(c) In the second year some selections of a universal character from the scriptures of the world be studied.

(d) In the third year, the central problems of the philosophy of religion be considered.

3. ***Primary Education***: Radhakrishnan praised M.K. Gandhi's scheme of basic education as a pattern for primary education in India. He said, "This education establishes contact of the student with everyday life. It explains the importance of physical education. The body is the means of the expression of human soul, therefore, physical education must be properly given."[21] He recommends teaching of both humanities and science subjects along with languages on the primary level.

4. ***Secondary Education***: Radhakrishnan has considered secondary education as a next step continuous with the primary

education. Therefore, on secondary stage also, the student should be provided a multisided curriculum including sciences, humanities and languages. The curriculum should be modified according to the needs of the country because the primary aim of education is to meet the needs of the nation and to create national unity. National unity may be created by teaching of history. Teaching of mathematics is necessary as it is on the primary stage as well. Agriculture and industrial arts and crafts should be taught so that the students may be capable of earning their livelihood. In India few people go to the institutions of higher education due to poverty and other causes. Therefore, presuming that most of the students will drop out after the secondary stage, they should be taught something of everything and also some useful craft to enable them to earn their livelihood.

5. ***University Education***: The most significant contribution made by Radhakrishnan to Indian education has been in the area of higher education. This contribution was made through the University Education Commission report. According to this report the objectives of the universities were as follows:

(i) To seek and cultivate new knowledge, to engage vigorously and fearlessly in the pursuit of truth, and to interpret old knowledge and benefits in the light of new needs and discoveries.

(ii) To provide the right kind of leadership in all walks of life, to identify gifted youth and help them develop their potential to the full by cultivating physical fitness, developing the powers of the mind and cultivating right interests, attitudes and moral intellectual values.

(iii) To provide society with competent men and women trained in agriculture, arts, medicine, science and technology and various other professions, who will also be cultivated individuals, imbued with a sense of social purpose.

(iv) To strive to promote equally and social justice and to reduce social and cultural differences through diffusion of education.

(v) To foster in the teachers and students, and through them in society generally, the attitude and values needed for developing the good life in individual and society.

(vi) To provide part-time and correspondence courses and extension programmes of various kinds so as to provide varied educational facilities for a widening clientele.

(vii) To undertake carefully worked out programmes for school improvement.

Radhakrishnan recommended selective admissions for institutions of higher education. He particularly laid emphasis upon research as the main aim of the universities. He favoured university autonomy in the selection of students, the appointment and promotions of teachers, the determination of syllabi, the methods of teaching and areas of research. He recommended establishment of an Inter University Board and the University Grants Commission. He recommended the establishment of at least one agricultural university in every State. He pointed out the need of reform in major universities. He analysed the problems of development of higher education in India. According to him the most important problems of higher education are:

1. Role of the university system, 2. Improvement of standards, 3. Restructuring of courses, 4. Post-graduate education and research, 5. Diversification of courses, 6. Decentralisation, 7. Autonomous colleges, 8. Academic freedom, 9. Medium of instruction, 10. Extension services, 11. Student discipline, 12. Role of UGC. Analysing all these problems Radhakrishnan made important recommendations. Among these recommendations, the most important, from the point of view of philosophy of education, are the recommendations concerning the role of university system in a nation. These recommendations sum up the aims and ideals of education according to Radhakrishnan. Therefore, it is necessary to enumerate these recommendations. They are as follows:

1. To inculcate and promote basic human values and the capacity to choose between alternative value system;
2. To preserve and foster our great cultural traditions and blend them with essential elements from other cultures and peoples;
3. To enrich the Indian languages and promote their use as important means of communication, national development and unity;

4. To promote a rational outlook and scientific temper;
5. To promote the development of the total personality of the students and inculcate in them a commitment to society through involvement in national service programme;
6. To act as an objective critic of society and assist in the formulation of national objectives and programmes for their realisation;
7. To promote commitment to the pursuit of excellence;
8. To promote the development of science and technology and of an indigenous capability to apply it effectively with special emphasis on national problems; and above all.
9. To contribute to the improvement of the entire educational system so as to sub-serve the community.

Medium of Education

Almost all the contemporary Indian philosophers of education have recommended mother tongue as the proper medium of education. Along with Sri Aurobindo and R.N. Tagore, Radhakrishnan raised his voice against making English the medium of instruction in India. Its biggest disadvantage is the formation of a class of educated persons which is cut off from the ordinary national at least from linguistic point of view. Such educated persons do not represent Indian culture since they imbibe western culture through the medium of English literature. The most natural medium of instruction for a child is his mother tongue. In India this credit should be given to regional languages. In spite of having an extraordinary mastery over English language, Radhakrishnan maintained, "It can never be seriously thought that English may ever become *lingua-franca* of India."[22] Pointing out the reason for it, he said that the Indians can never create great literature or original writings through English language. Psychological researches have approved that bilingualism is an impediment in the child's mental growth. It kills originality and creates confusion. Therefore, according to Radhakrishnan, a serious disadvantage of bilingualism in our education has resulted in the absence of originality. Along with regional languages Radhakrishnan also laid emphasis upon the study of Sanskrit since it is the repository of Indian culture. It is the language of Indian scriptures and lays down Indian philosophy of life. It is the medium through which the unity of nation may be preserved. Along with regional languages and Sanskrit, Radhakrishnan has accepted Hindi as an all India language. He accepts the three language formula in which the child is taught the mother tongue, the national language Hindi and the international language English. However, Radhakrishnan was against forcibly imposing Hindi on the people of South India. According to him, every State should make efforts for the growth of regional languages along with national language. Even on the question of script he admitted the rights of regional languages. He pointed out that Devanagri script should not be forcibly imposed upon others. The function of a language is to create bridges not to create gulfs. The University Education Commission, under the Chairmanship of Radhakrishnan recommended that the regional languages should be adopted as media of education at the university stage in phased programme spread over ten years. At the earlier stage of the undergraduate course, the bulk of the instruction may be given through the regional language while at the post-graduate stage, it may be in English. The teaching of important European languages other than English should be stressed, in particular the study of Russian, on a larger scale.

Teaching Methods

Radhakrishnan finds a place in the galaxy of great Indian teachers. Therefore, his views about teaching methods are not only theoretical principles but based upon actual experience of decades of teaching in Indian and Western universities. In his philosophy of education the teacher has been given a very honourable place in keeping with the ancient Indian philosophy of education. He recommends absolute freedom to the teachers in universities to follow such methods of teaching which they may deem fit for their purpose. According to Radhakrishnan, "The type of education which we may give to our youth, depends on the fact that what type of teachers we get."[23] The teachers should have a devotion to teaching besides their knowledge and scholarships. In ancient India the teacher was given highest status in the field of education and also in society since his life was as high as his ability. Most of the problems of the present system of education are due to failures of some teachers. In order to develop character in the educand the educator should himself develop his own character. According to Radhakrishnan, "The teachers have a special place in the formation of the mind and heart of our youth."[24] The teachers should have self-control and humanist standpoint. Great teachers in India have always preserved its culture, though many of them also travelled far and wide to know about other culture.[25] Thus, the teacher should be inquisitive. He should take interest in expansion of knowledge. As the Chairman of the University Education Commission Dr. Radhakrishnan insisted upon recruiting suitable teachers on various levels of education. The university teachers have the dual responsibility of character formation and research guidance. Therefore, while selecting them it is not only the scholarship but also their enthusiasm in character formation of the students which must be considered.

Proper teaching methods require proper teacher-taught ratio. Therefore, Radhakrishnan recommended that overcrowding at universities and colleges should be avoided. According to him the maximum number in the Arts and Science faculties of a teaching university should be 3,000 and in affiliated college 1,500. He recommended a minimum of 180 working days in a year exclusive of examination days. He was in favour of selective admissions to higher institutions. Along with reform of teaching method he suggested measures for student discipline. The teachers and students should carry out their part of the responsibility through intensive efforts to improve standards and the whole academic community should strive to serve society, through sustained, dedicated work and commitment to the pursuit of knowledge, excellence and national development. A nationwide effort should be organised to achieve a simultaneous breakthrough on the social as well as educational fronts.

Education for Different Sections of Society

In is a common knowledge that in contemporary Indian society all the sections were not given equal opportunities for education. The backward classes did not get sufficient opportunity even for acquiring primary education for their children. The woman education started only during the British period and even then the first girl to aspire for the graduation of Calcutta University had to seek special permission for it. As a teacher and as a Vice-Chancellor Radhakrishnan was very much conscious of this inequality. Therefore, he made particular reference to the education of those sections of society which have not been given sufficient opportunity. As the Chairman of The University Education Commission he made particular reference to women's education in the country. He pointed out that women students in general should be helped to secure their normal places in a normal society, both as citizens and as women, and to prepare for it. College programmes should be so designed that it will be possible for them to do so. The standards of courtesy and social responsibility should be emphasised in co-educational institutions.

In India it is a common knowledge that so many parents cannot send their wards for higher education due to economic difficulties. Referring to these sections of society, Radhakrishnan recommended enabling talented but economically weaker students to pursue their studies on a whole time basis by ensuring to them the full cost of their education, through appropriate bursaries, for which funds may be raised from public and private bodies.

Critical Evaluation

Among contemporary Indian philosophers of education Radhakrishnan had the longest and the most intimate experience of both college and university education, Indian and Western. Therefore, it is natural that his philosophy of education is most pragmatic. As the Chairman of the University Education Commission was instrumental in planning the present higher education in India. Many of his recommendations have to be still worked out such as the idea of autonomous colleges. His recommendations were thorough and multisided and based upon solid philosophical foundations. They were guided by a basic integral approach avoiding all one-sidedness.

Radhakrishnan's philosophy of education is based upon sound psychological and sociological foundations. He has rightly considered every aspect of human personality to be valuable for development. He aimed at the building up of integral spiritual human beings through education. In the tradition of ancient Indian philosophy of education he defined education as a process of character formation. Among values he laid emphasis upon democratic values and, therefore, asked for inculcation of liberty, equality and fraternity both among teachers and students.

Radhakrishnan's approach to aims and ideals, means, curriculum, school administration, etc., show an integral approach. He gave place to every subject in syllabi of education at different stages.

In the end, Radhakrishnan was a great humanist. He considered human freedom as the most valuable element to be safeguarded by the society and the state. He said, "Human personality is a sacred thing. He has a right that he should be considered an end in himself and, therefore, he has right to life, liberty and security."[26] The society should be organised in such a way that the freedom of the individual is curtailed only minimum. Basically there is hardly any contradiction between the interests of individual and society. However, if there is a contrast between the individuals and the society, the individual precedes the society. Every individual is a part of some social institution but he is also an individual with his personal sentiment, sense organs and never a means. He should be considered important and meaningful. "No State or institution should repress the individual."[27] The state is run by the individuals themselves. "State are alive due to individuals, dignity is the basis of faith in democracy."[28] Radhakrishnan showed reverence for man as it was shown by contemporary western humanists like Burtrand Russel along with contemporary Indian Humanists like Vivekananda, Sri Aurobindo, Rabindra Nath and M.K. Gandhi. As the President of Indian Rebublic he lost no opportunity to insist upon the preservation of individual freedom of the citizens. As a philosopher he considered the individual as a part of reality. His *Neo-Vedanta* philosophy nowhere overshadows the reality of the individual as it is seen in the thought of some contemporary Indian thinkers. Therefore, it was a fit foundation for constructing an integral humanist philosophy of education.

References

1. Radhakrishnan, S., *An Idealist View of Life* (London; George Allen & Unwin, 1947), pp. 15-16.
2. Radhakrishnan, S., *The Philosophy of Rabindra Nath Tagore* (Baroda: Good Companions, 1961), p. 101.
3. Radhakrishnan, S., *The Bhagvdgita*, p. 67.
4. Radhakrishnan, S., *An Idealist View of Life*, p. 153.
5. *Ibid.*, p. 147.
6. Arapura, J. G., *Radhakrishnan and Integral Experience* (Bombay: Asia Publishing House, 1966), p. 33.
7. Radhakrishnan, S., *The Hindu View of Life* (London: George Allen & Unwin, 1961), p. 256.
8. *Ibid.*
9. Muirhead and Radhakrishnan (Ed.), *Contemporary Indian Philosophy* (London: George Allen & Unwin, 1956), 2nd Ed., p. 492.
10. Radhakrishnan, S., *op. cit.*, p. 345.
11. Radhakrishnan, S., *Recovery of Faith*, pp. 89-99.
12. Schilpp, P. A., *The Philosophy of Sarvapalli Radhakrishnan* (The Tutor Publishing House, 1952), p. 27.
13. Radhakrishnan, S., *Kalki*, (Ludhiana: Kalyani Publishers, 1974), Sixth Ed., p. 37.
14. Radhakrishnan, S., *The Concept of Man* (London: George Allen & Unwin, 1960), p. 246.
15. Frankena, W.K. (Ed), *Philosophy of Education*, p. 54.
16. Radhakrishnan, S., *Speeches and Writings*, Vol, II, p. 267.
17. *Ibid.*, p. 259.
18. Radhakrishnan, S., *My Search for Truth* (Shivlal Agrawal), p. 20.
19. Radhakrishnan, S., *Recovery of Faith*, p. 158.
20. Radhakrishnan, S., *Speeches and Writings*, Vol. II, p. 175.
21. *Ibid.*, Vol. I, p. 249.
22. Radhakrishnan, S., *The Philosophy of Rabindra Nath Tagore*, (Baroda: Good Companions, 1961), p. 128.
23. Radhakrishnan, S., *Speeches and Writings*, Vol. II, p. 259.
24. Radhakrishnan, S., *op. cit.*, p. 202.
25. *Ibid.*, p. 204.
26. Radhakrishnan, S., *This is My Philosophy*, p. 315.
27. Radhakrishnan, S., *On Nehru* (New Delhi: Publication Division, Govt. of India, 1955), p. 24.
28. *Ibid.*

9

J. L. Nehru's Philosophy of Education

Jawahar Lal Nehru was born in a respectable and wealthy family during the period of national awakening. Consequently, his mind received the deepest impact of the evil consequences of World War I, the Home Rule League Movement inspired by Lokmanya Tilak and Mrs Annie Beasant, the Jallianwalla Bagh massacre and widespread public movements. This made him give up a life of leisure and jump wholeheartedly into the national movement for independence. It is from here that Nehru's political life was completely dominated by M.K. Gandhi, whom Nehru met for the first time during the Lucknow convention of the Congress in 1916. Nehru initially considered Gandhiji a non-political individual. However, gradually, Gandhi's influence on Nehru began to increase. It reached the high water mark of faith at the time when, in 1919, the Punjab Enquiry Commission was constituted.

Jawahar Lal Nehru's educational thought is influenced on the one side by such a western thinker as Karl Marx, and on the other by the ideas of Gandhi, though he never became a blind devotee of Gandhi. Their mutual relationship can be exemplified through the relationship between Plato and Aristotle. Aristotle, Plato's disciple, gave full respect to Plato and accepted his teacher's ideas, but he also differed from him on many essential points. In the same way, Nehru often criticized Gandhi very vehemently. In 1922, when Gandhi suspended the non-cooperation movement after the *Chaura-chauri* incident, Nehru was deeply chagrined. In the same way, Nehru did not owe the same allegiance to, or have faith in, the principle of non-violence as Gandhiji. He considered violence as a necessary tool both for maintaining peace in the country and ensuring its security.

Philosophical Foundations

Naturalistic Humanism

Although Jawahar Lal Nehru can be considered primarily a social and political thinker who did not take much interest in philosophy, it is an admitted fact that every thinker does formulate some philosophy of life, he invariably has his own conception of the sources and means of knowledge, validity of knowledge, the limits of knowledge, spiritual philosophy, soul, God and the universe. Nehru also had his own philosophy of life. The philosophical basis of his educational thought can be characterized as naturalistic humanism which, assumes Nature to be everything in place of God, and even in Nature gives to man the central place, thus aiming at human welfare as the supreme end.

The humanist thinker is rational, empirical and positivist. Nehru's theory of knowledge is a blend of all these three tendencies. Being a rationalist, Nehru wanted to submit every fact of life to the test of intelligence and reason. As a result, he had greater faith in science than in religion. He was an empiricist who wanted to establish the validity of every truth. Nehru tested philosophical assumptions on the basis of reason and experience, and like the positivists arrived at the conclusion that it is useless to cogitate upon philosophical problems. He was also opposed to religion, in the accepted sense of the word. The sole focus of his faith was man, and so he formulated the religion of humanity, substituting humanity for God.

The naturalistic bias of Nehru's humanism is made explicit by his attitude towards religion. He argued that any religion which was founded on blind faith, superstition, reaction, exploitation and vested interests was an impediment to national unity. And, in fact, most of the religious sects in the world of religion possess these characteristics. That is why Nehru has consistently criticized organised religion of every kind. He also disliked mysticism because in his view it was mysterious, concerned with the other world and inclined to demand a complete suspension of national thought, he favoured a scientific viewpoint towards religion, and so he was compelled to criticize it. It is clear that Nehru hatred for religion originated in some personal factor. His thoughts constantly reiterate the impression that some experiences in his life destroyed his faith in religion. It is reported that once, when he went to Sevagram to meet Gandhi, Smt. Kasturba Gandhi invoked divine blessings on him, praying that God may bless him with happiness. Nehru is reported to have retorted with an enquiry about where did God live. He also humorously remarked that if God really existed then He must be living in the profoundest sleep. Such anecdotes indicate that his personal experience made him see religion as based almost completely on superstition and exploitation.

In view of these facts and ideas, Nehru was a proponent of secularism. Clarifying his views, he declared that fundamentally, he believed in the present life, the present world, not in an imaginary future world. Whether there is such a thing as the world, or whether there was a life after death or not bothered him not at all. Nehru had come to believe that the world of today had no need of religion. In fact, he felt religion had more harm than good to offer, and so the world could progress faster and further by abandoning it. Here, Nehru's views can be said to manifest naturalistic humanism. Though he is an opponent of religion, his views repeatedly manifest humanist leanings, on the basis of which some scholars have tried to establish that Nehru was religious, though in his own individual and uncommon way.

In his later works, Nehru does not appear such a vehement critic of religion or God. In fact, at certain places he gives the impression of being a supporter of religion. In fact, Nehru did not oppose religion; his opposition was directed mainly at superstition and blind faith. He wanted to maintain a rational and scientific outlook on life, and consequently, he could not accept any mysterious viewpoint. So, Nehru should be seen as an opponent of blind faith or of a superstitious religion.

However, Nehru felt that by supporting or instilling superstitions, religion has only obstructed human progress. In his *Autobiography*, Nehru admitted that *Gita* has immeasurably benefited human society. His thoughts bore the influence of the teachings of the *Gita,* one copy of which almost never left his side. Many of his intimate companions regarded him as a deeply religious. According to Dr. Radhakrishnan, Nehru was not a religious man in the sectarian sense but he had the deepest faith in spiritual values. He was hostile to ritualism and adherence to religious dogmas, but he accepted truth and sympathy as supreme human values. If religion were regarded as a deeply faithful quest for truth in which the individual is willing to sacrifice his all, he was willing to list himself as one of the soldiers in the glorious army of religion.

Jawahar Lal Nehru did not evince any faith in any God with form who possessed, or was, a mysterious power. However, he accepted the consciousness of the Infinite. He also admitted that human knowledge is finite. But, in spite of this he could not bring himself to subscribe to many of the traditional beliefs of Hindu religion, such as the concept of the soul, the identity of the soul and God, etc. Yet, he was catholic enough to accept that religion does satisfy one of man's basic urges, without which it could not have been such a mighty force as it has through the ages, nor could it have granted solace to countless disturbed, agitated and restless souls, which also undoubtedly it has done. Nehru has accepted that some form of faith is essential for maintaining enthusiasm and a sense of purpose in human life. Under the influence of F.T. Brooks, he even came to have faith in Hindu religion, *Upanisads* and the *Gita*. This development was further strengthened by Gandhi's influence. Consequently, Nehru came to state that in 1921 he came nearest to a religious attitude that even in his childhood.

Importance of Education

Jawahar Lal Nehru has accepted education as the most important means to social change. His attitude towards education was scientific and worldly. Political thinkers and educational philosophers the world over admit that it is not possible to establish a democratic society successfully without an adequate and suitable system of education. Jawahar Lal Nehru was of the same opinion. In consequence, he stressed the fact that, "Only through right education can a better order of society be built up."[1] Being a socialist, Nehru attaches particular significance to the social objectives of education. According to him, "Education is the most important requisite to open up the individual."[2] "Freedom from ignorance is as essential as freedom from hunger."[3] Education is the means to socialization, it is the tool which trains citizens in the art of thinking. According to Nehru, the problems of a country cannot be solved merely through economic and political reform, since they require improved human relations also. Social development is inconceivable without mental development and a broadening of mental horizon. As a result, the major purpose of education is the victory of the mind and soul over lifeless matter. Nehru said, "Unless this conflict of the spirit is solved there is going to be no peace in any country."[4]

Aims of Education

Nehru's views on the aims of education bear resemblance to Rabindra Nath's ideas because both of them were firm internationalists and humanists. In his address to the students of Allahabad University, Jawahar Lal Nehru said, "A university stands for humanism, for tolerance, for reason, for the adventure of ideas and for the search for truth."[5] More or less the same words were repeated by Rabindra Nath when *Visva-Bharati* was established. Like other contemporary thinkers, Nehru too has stressed the spiritual aspect of social development. He said, "Without that spiritual element, probably the disintegration of society will proceed in spite of all material advance."[6] Clarifying Nehru's humanistic conception of education, K.G. Saiyedain remarks, "His interest in education stems basically from his interest in people, for, what is a good social order but the means for nurturing a good human personality?"[7] Because of his socialistic bias, Nehru explained the social objectives of education in human development thus, "When we consider the whole subject of education we have to think in terms of the state and the society we are aiming at; we have to train our people to that end; we have to decide what our citizens should be like and what their occupations should be . . we have to produce harmony and equilibrium in their private and social and public life."[8] He expressed his admiration for the Russian system of education in the following terms, "The object aimed at is to produce a desire to serve the community as a whole and to apply the knowledge gained not only for personal but for public welfare."[9]

Means of Education

Nehru tried to establish a system of education in India comparable to the West. The objective of his education was to do away with such narrow viewpoints as linguism, communal ism, religiosity, etc., and to generate in people a viewpoint which was scientific, humanistic, materialistic and ethical. An education of this kind alone can bring about the desired social change in the country. Welcoming English or British education into India, Nehru had remarked, "English education brought a widening of the Indian horizons ... a revolt against some customs and aspects of Indian life, and a growing demand for political reform."[10] This system of education represented exactly the system that Nehru wanted for India. He said, "I am all for opening our minds to every kind of knowledge and information that can be obtained. I am all for free intercourse with the rest of the world."[11]

Education is a safeguard against narrow-mindedness of all kinds. The economic objectives of education are as important as its social purposes because while on the one side it must aim at man's cultural improvement, on the other it must enable him to generate wealth in society. As Jawahar Lal Nehru put it, "What is important is that each person should produce something of value to society. Each one of you consumes what society produces by way of food, clothing and so on unless you produce the amount you consume you are a burden to society."[12] For this, as Nehru realized, the country had dire need of practical, scientific and technical education. It is because of this that Nehru laid so much stress on formulating an educational strategy for the independent India of the future. He declared, "In particular we want a system which can train the right type of personnel for the speedy exemption of development plans."[13]

Types of Education

Basic Education

Being Gandhi's associate in the political field, Jawahar Lal Nehru welcomed Gandhi's concept of basic education because he believed that, "Real education . . . must be based on the actual environment and experiences of the child, and it must fit him for the work he will have to do in after life."[14]

Accepting the importance of manual skill in education, Nehru said, "The mind is stimulated thereby and there is a co-ordination between the activities of the mind and the hands."[15] Consequently, accepting the importance of basic education for India, Nehru said, "It is the most modern concept meant to make a person fit intellectually and otherwise."[16]

Basic education was considered important both because it was revolutionary and also relatively inexpensive. In Nehru's words, "For a poor country like India with scores of millions of children to educate, the question of cost is important"[17] Elaborating the virtues of the Gandhian concept of basic education, Nehru eulogised thus, "It gives the child some cultural attainments, character and the capacity to work with his hands and to co-ordinate manual labour with mental and intellectual ability."[18] In this way, basic education was seen as a way out of the pervasive unemployment existing in the country.

Scientific and Technical Education

Nehru believed that industrialization was necessary for national progress in the economic fields because he was convinced that without the development of science and industry, the country could never be rid of poverty and unemployment. Consequently, he laid great emphasis upon the rapid growth of scientific and technical education in India. Being a humanist, he explained the scientific purpose of education by pointing out that by scientific developments, the minds of the rising generation may imbibe the spirit of science and be prepared to accept the new truth, even though it has to discard something of the old."[19]

Consequently, Nehru stated explicitly, that there is no future for us without science and technology. He regarded scientific and technical education as essential for the success of the nation's Five Year Plans. In this context, he said, "It would not be possible for us to go ahead with these plans unless there was a high standard of technical and scientific education."[20]

In the same way, this education was equally important for the nation's defense, because, as Nehru pointed out with great practical wisdom and foresight, "Strictly from the point of view of defence we have to go ahead rapidly with the production of trained people . . . engineers and the like . . . education will raise the level of our industrial effort and agricultural efforts."[21]

Thus, education is necessary for both peace and war. But this does not imply that Nehru wanted to thrust the values of the western industrialized world on India through scientific and technical education. In fact, he warned the nation against the pitfalls of industrialization when he said, "We should accept technology without leaving basic values which are of the essence of civilized man."[22]

Elaborating further he said, "Scientific and technical education will serve its purpose if it develops that humanistic spirit which is essentially one of tolerance, one of humanity, one of realization that somebody else may also have a bit of the truth."[23]

Cultural Education

In addition to scientific and technical education, Nehru regarded cultural education as equally important for the integral development of the human personality. From this viewpoint, he regarded education in literature, art and the humanities as of great significance. As he explained, "If that creative imagination is lacking, our growth becomes more and? more stunted, which is a sign of decay."[24]

In order to ensure that education in art and culture should grow rapidly in the country, Nehru advised that special institutions devoted to their propagation should be established in the country. He was himself the President of the *Sahitya Akademi*. It was his considered opinion that the state should have as little interference as possible in artistic, literary and educational activities. He said, "It is only when they manifestly become a social menace or a social danger that Government must move, and move with a firm determination."[25]

Education for Different Sections of Society

Nehru's viewpoint on the means and ends of education was comprehensive, integral, scientific and humanistic. Apart from cogitating upon the various aspects of education, he pointed cut the importance of making provisions for the education of the backward classes. His social ideas give a central place to the amelioration of the lot of the backward classes, and consequently, in education, he has given great importance to their education. Having seen the backwardness of Indian women he realized the need for their education. It is this which led him to elaborate that, "Women should be given the best of education in every department of human activity and be trained to play an effective part in all . . . spheres."[26]

Pointing to the role of mothers in the creation of an educated future generation, he said, "If you educate the women, probably men will also be effected since every educationist knows that the formative years of a person's life are the first seven or eight years."[27]

So in his opinion, women should be provided education and training, if not for their own sake, then for the sake of their children. He also pointed out that education would put women on the path to economic independence. He explained, "Everybody should be a producer as well as a good citizen and not a sponge on another person even though the other person may be one's own husband or wife."[28]

He felt that the provisions for education of women in the country must be extended to villages so that the rural sector should be made amenable to rapid social change. Nehru felt that the education of women was very important for the success of family planning and family welfare schemes. So, he pointed out that it is these girls who are likely to change the living habits of our people and will probably succeed in carrying this message of family planning further than some of the official plans.

As has been already made clear, Nehru stressed the importance of regional languages along with English as the media of education. The preceding analysis makes it amply clear that Nehru's thinking on education, like his thoughts on the other fields of thought, evinces a scientific, rational, progressive, liberal and humanistic attitude.

Critical Evaluation

Before examining Nehru's educational philosophy in details, it is desirable to understand clearly the difference between his ideas and that of Gandhi. The following is a brief account of their fundamental variance:

1. ***Concept of Religion and Faith in it***: Gandhi was, by nature, a very religious individual whereas Nehru subscribed to the ideal of secularly. Gandhi openly praised Hindu religion, while Nehru has rarely indulged in such encomiums. Gandhi has repeatedly stressed the virtues of religion but practically overlooked its vices, while Nehru did the exact opposite. Despite this, the two thinkers appear to have quite common views regarding the fundamental elements of religion.

2. *Conception of Non-violence*: Gandhi believed that non-violence is the highest religion but Nehru did not have such abiding faith in it. He favoured non-violence because he saw it as the most appropriate means available to India in the existing circumstances. He was also attracted towards non-violence by the spectacularly successful use made of it by Gandhi. He also came to realize that non-violence is an active force. He agreed with Gandhi's arguments favouring non-violence, but on the other hand, he also believed that violence or the use of force was necessary both for maintaining internal peace within the country and also for securing it against external invasion. He consistently refuted the Gandhian thesis that non-violence is truth because he saw the non-violent state as contrary to both logic (or rational thought) and science. In this way, Nehru visualizes the use of force as unavoidable in the life of society and the state.

3. *Difference in the Basis of Humanism*: Both Gandhi and Nehru were humanists but their views were rooted in different sub-strata. Gandhi's humanism had its root in his religious sentiment and faith in God while Nehru's conception was based on his implicit faith in man's innate power and potential. He had the deepest sentimental faith in mankind and believed in the ideal of a single, united world. He had profound faith in man's innate greatness. Thus, while Gandhi's humanism is essentially religious, Nehru's humanism may be considered scientific and ethical.

4. *Concept of the Welfare State*: The Gandhian concept of the welfare state differs considerably from Nehru's, since Nehru did not conceive of it as a non-violent state, which Gandhiji did.

Besides, he wanted to base it on secularism, not on any specific religion. His viewpoint was more realistic.

5. ***Industrial Policy***: Gandhi was a staunch opponent of big industry, because of which he wished to establish small and cottage industries in the country. In contrast, Nehru favoured modern science, and believed that the importance of large scale industry in eliminating poverty could not be denied. In his famous work *Discovery of India*, he wrote, "What I object is the craze for machinery and not machinery as such. If we could have electricity in every village home, I shall not mind villagers plying their implements and tools with electricity."[29]

6. ***Relationship between Means and Ends***: Although both Gandhi and Jawahar Lal Nehru subscribed to the view that both means and ends must possess identical moral probity, Nehru admitted that exceptions to the role were also important, Gandhi in contrast, could not countenance any such violation of the principle. His thoughts having been influenced by Gandhi on the one side and Karl Marx on the other, Nehru has spoken in favour of revolution at certain places.

7. ***Concept of the Ideal State***: Gandhi entitled his ideal state '*Ram Rajya*', but Nehru objected to the view because it carried clear overtones of a profound faith in Hindu religion, though he did not lay any great stress on this objection. Apart from this, their respective conceptions of the ideal state can be seen differing in respect of the importance of non-violence, the use of force, small and large industries and many other elements.

8. ***Effect of the East and the West***: Gandhi was devoted to Eastern thought whereas Nehru's mind was more profoundly coloured by Western ideas because of his education at Cambridge University which had understandably formed and shaped his mind. Because of this, Nehru wanted the nation to move ahead according to the ideas of progress imbibed from the West. On the other hand, Gandhi gave his allegiance to traditional Indian values, and wanted to prevent the nation from going the western way.

9. ***Difference in Social Ideals***: Elaborating on the differences between the social ideas of Nehru and Gandhi, Abid Hussain has explained that on comparing the social ideals of Nehru and Gandhi we find that in spite of many common elements, that

are notable differences in structure and force, and as a result, all the conceptions appear to be completely different. Both have profound faith in freedom and equality, but Gandhi lays greater emphasis on freedom while Nehru stresses equality. In the final analysis, these differences stem from the basic difference between the religious and the secular viewpoints.

Gandhi's thinking started from the individual whereas Nehru gave primacy to the welfare state. In his concept of trusteeship, Gandhi has visualized a change of heart among capitalists but Nehru rejected any possibility of this, and so his economic views could not accommodate the theory of trusteeship.

Despite the wide range of differences between the ideas of Gandhi and Nehru explained above, a close similarity between their thoughts on non-violence, democracy, welfare state, opposition to communalism, eradication of untouchability, nationalism and internationalism can be seen.

Our discussion of the educational philosophies of Vivekananda, Sri Aurobindo, Dayananda, Rabindra Nath and M.K. Gandhi in the earlier chapters of this work show an unanimity of opinions in the philosophy of education. These philosophers agreed upon metaphysical basis, integral viewpoint, integral psychology, spiritual explanation of human nature, multi-sided curriculum, mother tongue as the medium of education, synthesis of nationalism and internationalism in education and the value of *Brahmacarya*. They advocated education for all the sections of the society. They agreed that education aimed all round perfection of the educand. They wanted to build a spiritual society through education. Their educational philosophy was based upon *Neo-Vedanta* metaphysics. Jawahar Lal Nehru, on the other hand, was an educational thinker brought up in the western tradition. He had neither knowledge nor devotion to ancient Indian thought. His humanism was naturalistic, in contrast to the idealistic humanism of other contemporary Indian educational thinkers. Therefore, no wonder that his explanation of the aims of education was different from explanations advanced by other contemporary Indian philosophers of education. Impressed by the scientific progress of the west and the value of English education, Nehru supported the educational means prevalent in the west and planned to establish western type of education in India. This makes him the architect of the modern educational system in India. It was purely due to his regard for Gandhi that he supported Gandhian schemes of education. Left to himself, he would have planned a different system of education even for the rural India. He had no patience with superstitions, religious or otherwise. He was a positivist and atheist. At every stage of education, primary, secondary, university, Nehru visualised western aims and means. This is his weakness and this again is the strength of his philosophy of education.

In fact no one can deny that an ideal system of education in the present day India requires a synthesis of ancient Indian values and modern western means and techniques of education. Therefore, the value of educational philosophy of Jawahar Lal Nehru is clear. Like the western thinkers he aimed at all round development of the educand and never admitted salvation as the aim of education. A strong votary of technology and science he planned in a big way for the expansion of scientific and technical education in the country. His speeches to the students and teachers are more forthright, clear and unambiguous than many of the other contemporary Indian thinkers.

References

1. Nehru, J.L., *Soviet Russia,* p. 85.
2. Nehru, J.L., *Speeches,* Vol. IV, p. 183.
3. *Ibid.*
4. Nehru, J.L., *Independence and After,* p. 143.
5. Ibid.
6. Nehru, J.L., *Speeches,* Vol. IV, p. 169.
7. Zakaria, R. (Ed.), *A Study of Nehru,* p. 395.
8. Nehru, J.L., *Eighteen Months in India*, p. 284.
9. Nehru, J.L., *Soviet Russia,* p. 94.
10. Nehru, J.L., *The Discovery of India,* p. 337,
11. Nehru, J.L., *Speeches,* Vol. II, p. 72.
12. *Ibid.,* Vol. III, p, 405.
13. *Ibid.*
14. Nehru, J.L,, *Soviet Russia,* pp. 86-87.
15. Nehru, J.L., *Discovery of India*, p. 43.
16. Nehru, J.L., *Speeches,* Vol. IV, p. 163.

17. Nehru, J.L., *An Autobiography*, p. 604
18. Nehru, J.L., *Speeches,* Vol. III, p. 406.
19. Nehru, J.L., *India Today and Tomorrow*, p. 4.
20. Nehru, J.L., *Speeches,* Vol. III, p. 422.
21. *Ibid.,* Vol. IV, p. 149.
22. *Ibid.,* p. 170.
23. *Ibid.,* Vol. III, p. 433.
24. *Ibid.,* Vol. II, p. 383.
25. *Ibid.,* Vol. III, p. 409.
26. Nehru, J.L., *Recent Essays and Writings*, p. 146.
27. Nehru, J.L., *Speeches,* Vol. III, p. 398.
28. Nehru, J. L., *Discovery of India,* p. 356.
29. *Ibid.*

10

M. N. Roy's Philosophy of Education

The foundation of the educational philosophy of M.N. Roy is rooted in Radical Humanism. Radical humanism is, neither materialism nor idealism but a scientific philosophy insisting upon the freedom of the individual. The function of philosophy, according to M.N. Roy, "is to explain existence as a whole."[1] Distinguishing between the function of philosophy and science, Roy said, "The function of science is to describe; that of philosophy is to explain. Therefore, philosophy is called the science of sciences."[2] Thus philosophy, according to Roy, should be based upon scientific foundation. According to him, "Modern scientific philosophy is decidedly opposed to any, dualist doctrine."[3] Again it is against mysticism. "Mysticism' results from ignorance,"[4] said M.N. Roy. It implies an admission of defeat. Roy is against all brands of mysticism, metaphysical, logical or spiritual. According to him, "General laws of science have philosophical validity."[5] Science gradually explains philosophical problems. Scientific knowledge is the result of scientific method. These methods utilise experience and reason. Scientific investigation, according to Roy, "must place ontology before epistemology."[6] In the world view of M.N. Roy being and becoming both are important. "Becoming is the essence of being."[7] The world, according to Roy is dynamic. Therefore, it is becoming, change and evolution. Criticising absolute idealism, Roy said, "Absolute idealism is a double-edged sword.

It throws matter out of the front-door only to let it in by the back-door."[8] Noumenon as well as phenomenon are projections of our consciousness. Consciousness is the soul of reality. Roy has condemned subjective; approach to reality.

The metaphysical theory of the educational philosophy of M.N. Roy may be called materialistic monism or monistic naturalism. While according to the former, matter is the only ultimate reality, according to later the ultimate reality is Nature. Thus the philosophy of M.N. Roy is monistic. As has been already pointed out, Roy considered dualism to be the greatest difficulty faced by the philosophers. On his part he presents a philosophical view which involves the latest findings of physical and social sciences. The values, according to Roy, cannot be derived from the facts. They are self-evident and no less objective than facts. The ultimate reality is Nature or Matter. From matter has gradually evolved life and from animal life has evolved man. Therefore, man according to Roy, is biological. The humanist ethics is evolutionary.

Aims of Education

The aim of life is to live. Struggle for existence is the basic drive in organism. Thus Roy believes in Darwinian theory of evolution. The highest value in the human world is liberty. Our aim is to establish a social system which finds maximum freedom for the individual. Value cannot exist apart from man. Knowledge, truth, liberty are meaningful only in human context.

Thus the world view of M.N. Roy is man-centered. Man has the central position in cosmos. According to the rule 1 of Radical humanism, "Man is the archetype of society, co-operative social relationships contribute to develop individual potentialities. But the development of the individual is the measure of social progress."[9] Explaining social progress Roy laid down the 2nd principle "Quest for freedom and search for truth constitute the basic urge of human progress."[10] Making liberty of man the basic search in progress Roy said, "The purpose of all rational human endeavor, individual as well as collective, is attainment of freedom, in ever increasing measure."[11] The peculiar trait of man is his rationality. Man can make the world better with the help of science. Thought and environment interact. Real revolution requires full freedom of the individual. Therefore, Roy rejects the economic interpretation of history advanced by Karl Marx. Man according to him, is not an economic being but a moral being. Intellectual and spiritual life are conditioned by instinct of reason. According to Roy, "The residue of humanness, therefore, is the biological heritage of reason. To put the same thing differently, human nature is not to believe, but to struggle for freedom and search for truth, the latter aspect manifesting itself in *homo sapiens.* "[12] Morality is not directly derived from religion. Even the savage has a strong sense of good and bad. The quest for freedom distinguishes man from animals. Truth is a matter of human experience. Man's struggle for freedom is guided by his knowledge of nature. According to Roy, "The search for truth, therefore, is intimately associated with the quest of freedom as the essence of human nature."[13] This is the fundamental principle in the educational philosophy of M.N. Roy.

Aim of Society

According to Roy there can be no other purpose of life than living. Thus human life aims at expression of human processes. Since human society is constituted by human beings, therefore, its purpose is to serve the purposes of individuals. Thus human life itself is the aim of human collectivity. Since man has evolved out of the animal, therefore, the purpose of human life may be initially interpreted in biological terms. Struggle for existence is the first purpose of human beings. The human society makes the individual well-versed in this study. The human reason contributes for the efficiency in this struggle for existence. The aim of education is to manifest the unmanifested capacities of human individuals inherited as a biological organism. The reason has developed in the struggle for survival and the powers of judgment have evolved. This evolution has further led man to the moral level. The capacity of judgment is the basis of ethics and all moral values. Thus the struggle for survival together with conscious and rational efforts becomes the urge for liberty. The struggle for survival is waged in an environment. Efficiency in it requires all the instruments of struggle. The society is the outcome of man's urge to *liberty* since without it the individual alone could not face natural calamities. He needed the co-operation of others for hunting, agriculture and many other pursuits. It is hence that individuals combined to form society. Thus the only aim of society is to help the individual. Any social organisation which is an impediment to the free growth of the individual frustrates the very purpose for which it has been created. Therefore, there is hardly any contradiction in social organisation and liberty of the individual. In fact there is hardly any problem in the relationship of the individual and collectivity. This problem is the result of the false notion that the collectivity is above the individual or that it has any purpose different from the purpose of its constituents. If it is understood that the collectivity has no purpose apart from the purpose of the individual the controversy never arises.

The above mentioned principle may be used for the interpretation of the aim of education. The first and foremost need of man is to maintain physical existence. But, gradually as the society became more and more complex, the intellectual, moral and spiritual needs manifested. Man is the representative of society and requires social relationships for the development of individual capacities. The individual development is the criterion of social development since the individual is prior to collectivity. The moral traits like liberty, progress, welfare, etc., are first achieved by the individuals. In the end any welfare is ultimately individual welfare. There is no separate welfare of the collectivity. In the words of Roy, "Collective well being is a function of the well being of individuals."[14]

Explaining liberty as the aim of education Roy said, "The purpose of all rational human endeavor, individual as well as collective, is attainment of freedom in ever increasing measure. Freedom is progressive disappearance of all restrictions on the unfolding of the potentialities of individuals, as human beings, and not as cogs in the wheels of a mechanised social organism."[15] According to the third principle of democracy the freedom of the individual is the only aim of the collectivity of the state. As has been already pointed out, reason is the fundamental characteristic of human nature. Along with reason man has been endowed with emotions. The human will is the most potent element in human society. It is the determinant of human history. Marxist economic interpretation of history is born out of dualism. It is true that history is a determined process but the factors determining it are not one but many, of which human will is an important factor. Therefore, according to the third principle of radical humanism the only purpose of the collectivity and the state is the liberty of the individual. It is clear that man's freedom is the highest moral standard according to radical humanist ethics. In the words of M.N. Roy, "The axiology of Radical Humanism deduces from the supreme value of life, because the urge for freedom is the essence of human existence."[16] In the process of evolution, according to Roy, moral values have evolved out of the animal traits. Radical humanist ethics does not require any religious or trans-mundane basis. In the words of Roy, "To be moral, one needs only to be human; it is not necessary to go in search of divine or mystic-metaphysical sanction. Humanist morality is evolutionary."[17]

Humanist educational values have evolved out of human needs. Besides liberty Roy refers to other values. To quote his own words, "The hierarchy of humanist axiology, thus, is freedom, knowledge, truth. They are not autonomous; they are inter-related, logically as well as ontologically."[18] Thus liberty and goodness are intimately related. So are related knowledge and virtue. Reminding the ancient Greek Socratic ethics Roy said, "Therefore, freedom cannot be attained by immoral means, nor can an enlightened man be a liar."[19]

Value of Reason

Reason, according to Roy is the basic trait of human being. This reason is the determinant of history as well as economics. Revolution according to Roy requires economic reorganisation for the provision of maximum liberty to everyone. To quote his words, "For creating a new world of freedom, revolution must go beyond an economic reorganisation of society. Freedom does not necessarily follow from the capture of political power in the name of the oppressed and exploited classes and abolition of private property in the means of production."[20] Again, a moral order will result from a rationally organised society, because, viewed in the context of his rise out of the background of a harmonious physical Universe, man is essentially rational and, therefore, moral. Education fulfils the rational desire for harmonious and mutually beneficial social relations.

Means of Education

In his work, *Politics, Power and Parties*, M.N. Roy has elaborated his educational thought. Like Plato he insists that no ideal republic can be established in the absence of educated persons. According to him so long as the individuals are unable to distinguish between right and wrong no good society can be established. In other words, an ideal society is constituted by rational men and women. This rationality is a characteristic found everywhere. According to Roy it is scientific knowledge that every human being possesses reason and rational thought, a characteristic of intelligence, a trait of human nature."[21] Therefore, what is required is to encourage reason in man. This is possible only through education. According to Roy those who want to put democracy in practice should feel that democracy is impossible without education.[22]

Here education does not mean literacy nor compulsory primary education. Roy is against any compulsion in education because compulsion is against liberty. Criticising the prevalent system of education, Roy pointed out that what is required is a different type of education. An education which seeks to maintain the *status quo* is not suitable for making the community conscious of its inherent powers. Education should help men and women to think rationally and to decide themselves, about the problems to be solved. Roy lamented that no government provides such an education. Almost all the governments in the world aim at creating mental slavery through education. The state governed education, teaches the masses to sing songs of patriotism to salute the national flag, to study the history edited by Government, and to work collectively to achieve success of the state. Therefore, the demand of the state governed education is suicidal in backward and underdeveloped countries. No national education provided by government in any country is the true democratic education.

Types of Education

Education of Citizenship

In his radical social thought Roy has considered education the foundation for democracy since it is only through it that rational individual may be created. Clarifying the aim of his new system of education Roy pointed out that believing in the modern scientific knowledge that man is basically rational, we will attempt to arouse rationality of all the citizens. This is the aim of education.[23] Once this process of education is started, other steps may be taken for the establishment of democracy because every such step requires rational judgment. According to M.N. Roy education of the citizens is necessary for the establishment of scientific politics in place of party politics. He maintained that the education of the citizens and the gradual building up of a political organisation from below is the only guarantee against the dangers of party system.[24] Further clarifying this guarantee Roy pointed out that scientific education will make people self-dependent, rational and distinctive, and, therefore, they will not be further hypnotised for any evil purpose. It will give birth to a new institutional organisation which will be a guarantee against exploitation by an individual or a group of individuals.[25]

Political Education

Thus the expansion of education will make the citizen oppose all sorts of exploitation by an individual or a group. In the present situation victory in elections is not the proof of a party of being democratic since most of the voters are uneducated and cannot oppose the political party in power. It is only through education that the public will rise to oppose any immoral or inadequate political party and may not allow it to come in power again. Thus humanist politics is ultimately based upon education.

Education of Freedom

Explaining his democratic new educational system Roy pointed out that as a pre-condition of democracy education is not primary education nor is it traditional higher or scientific education. It is the process of raising the intellectual and cultural level of the mass.[26] Therefore, so long as the moral and cultural level of the people does not rise, the aim of education is not realised. The education provided in so-called parliamentary democracies is not the education of freedom but an education of slavery. These states provide compulsory free primary education to create citizens supporting the state and not free individuals. According to M.N. Roy, new humanism expresses a new viewpoint towards the problems of education which suggests that given opportunity every human being has the capacity to develop his abilities to an unlimited extent.[27] According to new humanism it is not in the interest of the government or the State to curb the citizen's freedom to grow their capacities because ultimately a welfare state aims at making its citizens more and more free. The aim of education is not merely to provide three R's but to create among the people a consciousness towards humanity, consciousness towards its right to be human beings and consciousness of its excellence and dignity. The purpose of education is to help them in utilising their reason in this thinking.[28] It is only such an education which may create true democracy not only in a nation but in the whole world. This educational system, however, as has been already pointed out, will be run not by the government but by the public itself.

Education for Different Sections of Society

According to M.N. Roy the basic difficulty with the present society is the suppression of individual freedom. Social justice requires that all individuals must be free and equal. Roy is not satisfied by merely establishing political democracy. He pleads for economic social democracy. The essential conditions of success of democracy according to him is the creation of free individuals. This can be done by means of education. The education must be equally available to all the sections of society. Roy condemns the ancient Indian distinction between male and female, *Brahmin* and *Sudra* regarding the facility of education. His spiritualism is anti-traditionalism. Therefore, he strongly condemns any distinction between different sections of society based upon political, economic or social considerations. The aims and ideals of education can be achieved only by realisation of human values and the establishment of a humanist society. The sole aim of the state is to help in the achievement of this aim. Therefore, the state must arrange for the education of different sections of society. This requires additional help to backward sections since they are lagging behind other sections of society. During Roy's time sufficient facility of education was not available to females and backward classes in India. Along with most of his contemporary Indian philosophers of education

Roy raised his voice against this inequality. The credit of the vast expansion of education among these sections of Indian society goes as much to Roy as to other contemporary Indian philosophers of education.

Critical Evaluation

Thus, according to M.N. Roy, "The crisis of modern civilisation, in the last analysis, therefore, is a spiritual crisis."[29] Man today has lost faith in himself. Everywhere worship of group and collectivity has become a religion. All political parties worship power in which political leaders are the priests and the masses follow them blindly. Thus humanist values have been lost in modern culture. The humanist movement of M.N. Roy was not only for India but for the whole world. As he said, "Our appeal is to reason and moral responsibility. The response to this entirely disinterested appeal will be the measure of hope for the future not only of our country, but of the modern civilisation."[30]

New humanism is a scientific and integral philosophy. In it human being has been discussed not only in the context o society but in that of the whole cosmos. It is not an individualist philosophy though its central theme is the liberty of the individual. Individual and society, according to it, do not exist separately. The basic principles of Radical humanism have been laid down in the *Manifesto* of the Radical Democratic Party some of which have been already quoted in this chapter. According to the last principle of Radical Humanism, "Radicalism starts from the dictum that man is the measure of everything" (Protagoras) or 'man is the root of mankind' (Marx), and advocates reconstruction of the world as a commonwealth and fraternity of free men, by the collective endeavour of spiritually emancipated moral men."[31] New Humanism rejects the hypothesis that man is basically guided by faith. On the other hand, it supports the scientific concept that man is basically rational in nature. Therefore, each human being is capable of attaining knowledge and solving individual and social problems. New Humanism makes morality the basis of educational philosophy since moral values are the chief values of human culture. Radical Humanism rejects fascist idea which is found in many so-called revolutionary social theories. Radical Humanism considers equality and liberty equally necessary. The easiest means for social change is making men and women moral. Radical Humanism does not distinguish between means and end and identifies them. It lays emphasis upon the present changes to make a bright future. Man himself is the revolutionary aim, and real education makes human being free. The formation of a new society will not be limited to space and time. It will be realised only when it is realised everywhere. Thus a real social revolution will be a world revolution.

References

1. Roy, M.N., *Science and Philosophy* (Calcutta: Renaissance. Publishers, 1947), p. 31
2. *Ibid.*
3. *Ibid.*, p. 34.
4. *Ibid.*, p. 25.
5. *Ibid.*, p. 37.
6. *Ibid.*, p. 45.
7. *Ibid.*, p. 47.
8. Roy, M.N., *New Humanism* (Calcutta: Renaissance Publishers. Pvt. Ltd., 1961), p. 51.
9. *Ibid.*
10. *Ibid.*, pp. 51-52.
11. Roy, M.N., *Reason, Romanticism and Revolution*, Vol. I, p. 23.
12. *Ibid.*, p. 32.
13. *Ibid.*, pp. 51-52.
14. Roy, M.N., *Radical Humanism,* p. 17.
15. *Ibid.*
16. *Ibid.*
17. *Ibid.*
18. Roy, M.N., *New Humanism* (Calcutta: Renaissance Publishers, 1961), p. 53.
19. Roy, M.N., *Politics, Powers and Parties*, p. 72.
20. *Ibid.*, p. 58.
21. *Ibid.*
22. *Ibid.*, p. 59.
23. *Ibid.*, p. 85.

24. *Ibid.*, p. 101.
25. *Ibid.*
26. *Ibid.*, p. 118.
27. *Ibid.*, p. 119.
28. *Ibid.*, p. 121.
29. Roy, M.N., *New Humanism*, p. 86.
30. *Ibid.*, p. 97.
31. *Ibid.*, p. 59.

11

Trends in Contemporary Indian Philosophy of Education: Concluding Remarks

The purpose of the present thesis is to analyse and summarise the trends in contemporary Indian philosophy of education. These trends show the directions towards which contemporary Indian philosophy of education is progressing. Thus, it sets the lines towards which one may look for interpretation of the various facets of contemporary Indian philosophy of education. On the other hand, it also lays down the broad principles on which a national scheme of education should be formulated. *Svadharma* has been the cherished principle of Indian philosophy since ancient to the present day. If a scheme of education has to be successful in this country it must be based upon the fundamental trends exhibited by contemporary Indian philosophers of education. Among the contemporary Indian philosophers of education J.L. Nehru and M.N. Roy show the discordant note, the influence of modern western thought upon Indian thinkers. Vivekananda, Sri Aurobindo, Dayananda, M.K. Gandhi, Rabindra Nath and Sarvapalli Radhakrishnan, on the other hand, follow the traditional Indian educational thought modifying and adjusting it in contemporary situations. This later group of thinkers, therefore, represents the Indian spirit in contemporary Indian philosophy of education. Our analysis of the contemporary trends will, therefore, be primarily based upon the educational thought of these traditionalist thinkers. Among the most important trends in contemporary Indian philosophy of education are: Revivalism, Rationalism, Humanism, rise of *Vedanta*, integralism, positivism, nationalism, cosmopolitanism, eclecticism, idealism, realism and pragmatism. After a brief analysis of these trends a possible synthesis will be attempted to arrive at an ideal philosophy of education for India today.

Revivalism

According to the Concise Oxford Dictionary, "Revival means bringing or coming back into use or vogue." Thus, revival seeks to bring again the ancient aims and ideals, means and concepts. Revivalism is the trend which shows a religious fervour, a reawakening, a reinterpretation in the light of the ancient wisdom. Therefore, revivalism is not a derogatory trend unless it refuses to acknowledge the present changes and to modify and adopt according to them. Such a revivalism can be seen in the philosophy of education of Vivekananda, Dayananda, M.K. Gandhi, Sri Aurobindo, Rabindra Nath and Radhakrishnan. All these thinkers have basically accepted the ancient Indian ideal of education as that which liberates the human soul out of the bondage. Thus, education seeks to set free the educand from all shackles of bondage. This, however, does not mean escapism or emphasis upon extra-terrestrial aim of life. All these thinkers pleaded for including ancient scriptures, the *Vedas*, the *Upanisads*, the *Bhagvadgita*, in the curriculum. All these thinkers laid emphasis upon close relationship of the teacher and the taught as has been hinted by the term *Upanisad*. All these thinkers praised the glory of ancient India, the ideals of *Rama* and *Sita,* the *Varna Asram* system, the *Purusarthas,* the theory of *Karma* and rebirth. Even while condemning casteism they praised the *Varna* system. However, they condemned the discrimination in the field of education as practiced by certain *Dharmasastras*. They did not accept the idea that women or backward classes are in any way inferior or that any educational disability can be imposed upon them. Therefore, they insisted upon the urgent need of the education of women and backward classes. All of them rejected classes and praised the masses. Their philosophy of education is fundamentally based upon the ancient Indian idea that one *Brahman* manifests in all the diversity of society and nature. Therefore, they insisted upon equality of opportunity for all in the field of education. This revivalism is also explicit in the patriotic and nationalist utterances of Vivekananda and Sri Aurobindo. M.K. Gandhi sought to revive the ancient Indian moral values of truth and non-violence in every field of life. Dayananda sought to bring back the ancient *Sanatan Dharma* to sway every field of life. Therefore, they recommend that contemporary Indian education should follow the ancient Indian ideals, values and models of social relationships, curricula, teacher-taught relationship, methods of teaching, etc. What requires change are the means of education. The modern means of education, the audio-visual instruments, the apparatus of modern science should be borrowed everywhere, particularly in the field of education of science and technology. Revivalism only craves for ancient ideals and values. It accepts modern means and mechanisms. Therefore, the revivalist tendency in contemporary Indian philosophy of education cannot be derogative.

Rationalism

The influence of western thinking, upon contemporary Indian thinkers is most explicit in the trend towards rationalism. All the thinkers, traditionalist as well as west-oriented agree about the value of reason in man's life and education. While J. L. Nehru and M.N. Roy place reason on the highest pedestal and openly and unconditionally support rationalism, Dayananda, Sri Aurobindo, Vivekananda, Rabindra Nath Tagore and Radhakrishnan follow the ancient tradition according to which while aims and ideals, goals and values are intuitive, the means are supplied by reason. Swami Dayananda, the great revivalist thinker proposes and adheres to the rationalist principle in the propounding of his famous work *Satyartha Prakash*. He promises that he will not accept anything which is not supported by reason. In India reason has never been taken as an opponent of intuition. The fields of intuition and reason have been clearly defined and none of the two is allowed to transgress another's field. Thus in the field of educational values, for example, intuition is the primary means while reason has to follow the dictates of intuition. Contrary to the western rationalism which makes reason a slave of passions, the Indian thinkers make it subordinate to intuition only and always superior to passions. The primary function of reason in this country has been to control the infra-rational passions and tendencies. Up to the mental level reason is the highest law but as one rises above mind reason has to bow its head and acquiesce. Thus the rationalist trend in contemporary Indian philosophy of education is a part of the fundamental integral approach. In the educational philosophy of J. L. Nehru and M. N. Roy, of course, one finds a tendency towards western type of rationalism, but at places they have also agreed about the value of intuition and other sources of human knowledge.

Humanism

The most important trend in contemporary Indian philosophy of education is humanism. The English word 'Humanism' has been derived from the Latin term '*Homo*' which means human being. Thus literally speaking, humanism is the philosophy in which man occupies a central place. Etymological meaning, however, is not the sufficient meaning of the term; it includes its historical usage as well. The use of a term in the historical tradition gradually unveils the different aspects of its meaning. Thus, in order to understand the full implication of the term 'Humanism' one must take into account its historical evolution. In this historical evolution, whatever has been found to be useful for human welfare has been attached to the concept of humanism such as the idea of social welfare, scientific attitude, progress of democratic institutions, etc. Like the West, humanism was born in India in ancient thought. Indian thought has its roots in the *Upanisads*. These *Upanisads* show humanistic trends. The *Bhagvadgita* is known as the essence of the *Upanisads*. The metaphysical postulates here are the same as found in the *Upanisads*. Indian philosophy after the *Upanisads* and the *Gita* had been a re-interpretation of the ancient philosophy according to changed circumstances and with difference of emphasis. Thus, the six philosophical system had their origin in the *Upanisads*. Not only these orthodox systems but also the heterodox systems as well had their origin in the *Upanisads*. Even the contemporary thinkers have developed their thinking on the basis of ancient

Upanisadic thought. Thus Sri Aurobindo, Vivekananda, Rabindra Nath, Gandhi and Dayananda have presented *Neo-Vedanta* Philosophy according to contemporary conditions in India and in the context of development of thought in the West and East. All these philosophers, with minor differences among them, have maintained what can be called integral humanism. This integral humanism is the philosophy of our age. It alone can supply the philosophical framework for the understanding of the problems of our society.

The humanist trend in contemporary Indian philosophy of education may be seen in Vivekananda's interpretation of the aim of education as man making. It is clear in Sri Aurobindo's ideal of superman as the aim of future education. It is explicit in Rabindra Nath Tagore's emphasis upon cosmopolitanism in education. Dayananda considered human welfare as the only ideal of the truth seeker, the teacher and the taught. Similar tendencies may be seen in the educational philosophy of Radhakrishnan. Humanism again sums up the educational philosophy of J.L. Nehru. M.N. Roy explicitly called his educational philosophy Radical Humanism. It should be remembered here that among these thinkers one finds two types of humanism. While J.L. Nehru and M.N. Roy support naturalistic humanism, borrowed from the West, Vivekananda, Dayananda, Sri Aurobindo, M.K. Gandhi and Radhakrishnan follow the Indian brand of humanism coming from the ancient *Vedas*, the *Upanisads*, and the *Bhagvadgita* This will be further clear by the analysis of the *Neo-vedanta* trend in contemporary Indian philosophy of education. While fundamentally, there is no essential difference between the Western and Indian humanism, the later is represented by the traditionalist group of Indian philosophers of education. Therefore, it is their humanism which forms the essential element of Indian philosophy of education.

Rise of Vedanta: Neo-Vedanta

Neo-vedanta, as is explicit from the very term, is the philosophy of *Vedanta* in the modern garb or the philosophy of *Vedanta* re-interpreted in the right of modern knowledge. As a consequent effect of this re-interpretation, the *Vedanta* philosophy has acquired a new and somewhat different form. In order to appreciate what is new in it and how is it linked with the ancient *Vedanta* it is called *Neo-Vedanta*. The philosophy, as expressed in the ancient philosophic treatises known as *Upanisads*, is known as the *Vedanta* philosophy. According to this philosophy, both the *quint essence* and *Summum genus* of all creation is *Brahman* and that *Brahman*, the Lord, is Infinite, Eternal, Omnipresent, Omnipotent and Pure Consciousness. He is the elan Vital or Soul of all. He is Truth, Existence and Consciousness. He is the sustainer of all creation. According to *Chandogya Upanisad, Brahman* is the creator, the destroyer and the sustainer of this world. The powers of Nature are part of His infinite power. All forces in the world are active through Him. According to *Taittariya Upanisad* all physical existence emerges out of Him, is merged into Him and is sustained by Him. According to *Chandogya Upanisad*, *Brahman* pervades all existence and is Omnipresent.

From the foregoing account of the *Vedanta* philosophy, it is plain that from the viewpoints of metaphysics, epistemology as well as axiology *Vedanta* is monistic, that is, it believes in one Supreme power behind everything. Thus, *Brahman,* soul and liberation are merely nominal variations of the same element. Most of the modern Indian philosophers also believe that creation is unity in diversity and that self, God and world are all expressions of one Supreme *Brahman*. Thus the views of these philosophers are closely akin to the *Vedanta* philosophy. Indeed the Indian philosophy from its very inception to modern times, has followed the basic tenets of the *Upanisadic* philosophy, barring, of course, the heterodox schools like Charvaka, Jainism, etc. The eminent Indian thinkers Vivekananda, M.K. Gandhi, Sri Aurobindo, Rabindra Nath Tagore and Dr. Radhakrishnan all have more or less dilated upon the themes found in *Upanisads*. If, to borrow a phrase from A.N. Whitehead, western philosophy is only footnotes' to Plato, the Indian philosophy can justly be said to be a commentary upon, the teachings of *Upanisads*.

From the foregoing account, it is clear that the modern Indian philosophy is rooted in the *Upanisadic* philosophy. But if the modern Indian philosophy is nothing but merely an elaboration of the *Upanisadic* teachings, then the question which would naturally crop up in everyone's mind is what is new in it and how and in what manners is it different from the ancient philosophy? What are its new characteristics which justify calling it new? For some historical reasons there was little philosophic thinking and development in India in the post-*Upanisadic* period. With the coming of the British and the consequent spread of the English language and western culture, a new awakening took place in the minds of Indian people and there was revival of active interest in our ancient philosophy and culture. Consequent upon the tremendous impact of western ideas and ways of life, many Indian thinkers rediscovered the ancient Indian wisdom, which they so reinterpreted as to harmonize with new scientific knowledge and technique. In this process of re-discovery and re-adjustment they were immensely aided by the yeoman efforts of the western orientalist. *Neo-vedanta,* succinctly, is nothing but the ancient *Upanisadic* wisdom re-interpreted in the light of modern science and technology and the western ideology. The philosophy which emerges out of this healthy fusion of forces is a salubrious *via* media between extremes of spirituality and asceticism and materialism and self-indulgence. This philosophy provides hope not only to the East but to the West also.

The *Neo-Vedanta* tendency is the basis of the aims and ideals propounded in contemporary Indian philosophy of education. It is again the basis of emphasis upon education of science and technology, the realistic interpretation of the world and the reformist trend. It is also the basis of spiritual nationalism preached by all the contemporary Indian philosophers. It is the basis of the synthesis of spiritual and material values. The spiritual interpretation of human nature advanced by Vivekananda, Dayananda, Sri Aurobindo, M.K. Gandhi and Radhakrishnan is due to *Neo-vedanta* trend. The fundamental postulate of *Neo-Vedanta* is unity in diversity. This has been the basis of multi-sided curriculum propounded by contemporary Indian philosophers of education.

Integration: Integralism

Our contemporary Indian philosophers of education Sri Aurobindo, Vivekananda, Rabindra Nath, Gandhi and Daya- nanda depict an integral approach in philosophy. "The work of philosophy", says Sri Aurobindo, "is to arrange the data given by the various means of knowledge, excluding none, and put them into a synthetic relation to one truth, the one supreme and universal reality."[1]

Thus, these philosophers believe in a monistic, idealistic, and integral philosophy. There is one Spirit underlying matter, life and mind in the world. This Spirit is the reality and man, Nature and God are its triple manifestation. In the words of Radhakrishnan, "It is the basis and background of our being, the universality that cannot be reduced to this or that formula."[2] This spirit evolves in the form of the universe. This evolution is not linear, dialectical or emergent but spiral. To quote Bhagwan Das, "The words '*evolution*' and '*involution*' embody, with instinctive correctness, the idea that these processes are forth and back, circling and cycling in a spiral."[3]

To realise this spirit Indian philosophers have utilised intuitive method. This is spiritual intuition, distinct from physical, mental or vital intuitions. According to Bhagwan Das, "It is the immediate condition or rather awareness of the self by the self, eternal self-consciousness."[4] In the words of Radhakrishnan, "The deepest things of life are known only through intuitive apprehension."[5] Thus contemporary Indian philosophers have advocated the use of intuitive method in order to arrive at an integral philosophy.

Contemporary Indian philosophers have looked to human personality from an integral perspective. They have maintained an integral theory of human nature. It is because of the integral human nature that Sri Aurobindo, Vivekananda, Rabindra Nath, Gandhi and Dayananda have advocated a multi-sided scheme of education including education for physical, mental, social, moral and religious development of the male and female. To formulate such a scheme of education, these philosophers borrowed both from ancient Indian wisdom and modern western scientific knowledge. This was the basis of the international universities founded by Rabindra Nath and Sri Aurobindo. In the words of Sri Aurobindo, "The aim and principles of a true national education are not certainly to ignore modern truth and knowledge but to take our foundations on our own belief, our own mind, our own spirit."[6]

Integral trend in education has led to a synthesis and harmony between education in science and humanities. Thus social studies such as economics, political science and sociology together with ethics find an important place in the curriculum because the integralist emphasises social more than individual aim of education. The teaching of science and mathematics is being more and more encouraged. On the other hand, this does not mean any setback to education of humanities. Thus, the integral curriculum includes literature and art. Writers and artists are given maximum freedom in an integral culture. Emphasis is laid upon folk culture and folk art. Thus the integral trend in education has led to almost a revolution about the aims and ideals, curriculum, extra-curricular activities, school administration and other fields of education.

Positivism

Positivists believe that through scientific method man will be able to control his environment, get leisure for culture pursuits and create a world more congenial to human life. Thus they have supported the growth of science everywhere. The Indian humanists, however, while admitting the value of science for human life, also point out to the dangers arising from science worship. Thus Sri Aurobindo, Rabindra Nath, Vivekananda and Gandhi have realised the value of technical education and the place of science in curriculum but at the same time insisted that the education of science and technology must be supported by education in humanities, art, morality and religion.

Nationalism

The most powerful expression of the nationalist tendency in education among contemporary Indian thinkers may be found in the educational theory of Swami Vivekananda and Sri Aurobindo. Both these thinkers called patriotism the highest religion. They almost worshipped their motherland. Their reformist schemes in education were inspired by love of the fellow countrymen. They asked the students to work hard and live for the country.

This nationalism, however, was spiritual nationalism and, therefore, in tune with internationalism. It is what Sri Aurobindo called 'Subjective Nationalism'. Therefore, it is free from all the defects of aggressive nationalism seen in the West. In fact it was based upon the ancient Indian ideal of *Svadharma*. According to this ideal, each nation and each human being has a particular status and role to perform in life. The humanity again has a *Svadharma* according to its nature. Everywhere, in man, nation and humanity the ideal is to follow the *Svadharma*. The idea of *Svadharma* also includes respect for the other's *dharma* and the understanding that for everyone his own *dharma* is the most sacred being based upon his fundamental nature. This spiritual nationalism inspired not only the aims and ideals but also the detailed outlines of the educational philosophies of Vivekananda, Dayananda, Sri Aurobindo and M.K. Gandhi.

Cosmopolitanism

Cosmopolitanism is the key note to understand the educational philosophy of Rabindra Nath Tagore, J.L. Nehru and M.N. Roy. The *Visva-Bharati* of Rabindra Nath was meant not only for India but for the world. The trend of cosmopolitanism was so much prominent in his educational ideas that some nationalist persons raised objections to it. The cosmopolitanism of J.L. Nehru has been well known. M.N. Roy everywhere stood for cosmopolitanism and hoped to make his Radical Humanist movement a world movement. The cosmopolitan tendency may also be seen in the educational philosophy of Vivekananda, Dayananda, Sri Aurobindo and Radhakrishnan though in their realistic thinking nationalist interests must be the educationists' foremost concern.

Eclecticism

The eclectic tendency in education implies the tendency to create an admixture of earlier tendencies. At least in the field of science and knowledge it has become evident that there is nothing entirely new, that even the most recent is a mixture of many earlier elements. A historical analysis of the present civilization will show that it is composed of numerous civilizations, which existed in the past. If one takes the example of India alone, one finds that the contemporary culture is a composite culture which clearly reflects the influences of the races living within the country, as well as the races which migrated to this country. Much the same can be said of other countries as well. Every nation is the outcome of the development of some earlier nation. The principle of evolution which is accepted by scientists today also proves that every new situation is the outcome of a mixture of earlier situations. Hence, in the sphere of education also people have come to believe that in the curriculum, teaching methods, aims of education, etc., we should achieve a mixture of the past tendencies so as to take advantage of the merits of each one. This is the reason why one finds elements of almost all the traditional methods in even the most recent method of teaching. Even in respect of the aims of education, there is a strong inclination in favour of integration of various aims and finding a synthesized aim. In other spheres also the adoption of such an attitude is looked at favourably. This is the eclectic tendency in education. It can also be called the tendency of compromise or the completion. Undoubtedly, the eclectic tendency is better than the one sided view because it is more comprehensive, liberal and extensive.

The contemporary Indian philosophers of education have looked to human personality from an eclectic perspective to discover the inner kernel which is often missed by social sciences. They emphasise the spiritual aspect of man as an integrating principle which alone can boost his future evolution. It is because of an eclectic theory of human nature that Sri Aurobindo, Radhakrishnan, Tagore and Gandhi have advocated an eclectic scheme of education including physical, moral and religious education true to the spirit of Indian culture, in spite of incorporating latest scientific truths. "The aim and principles of a true national education," said Sri Aurobindo, "is not certainly to ignore modern truth and knowledge but to take our foundations on our belief, our mind, our own spirit."[7]

Thus contemporary Indian philosophy of education has been characterised by eclecticism. This is because most of its spokesmen, including Aurobindo, Radhakrishnan, Vivekananda, Gandhi and Tagore had a wide and deep knowledge of western science, art, literature and culture and a firsthand contact with the West. It is hence that they could compare Eastern thought with Western and reach at an eclectic viewpoint. Thus one finds a meeting of idealism and realism, ancient Indian ideals and modern western principles, nationalism and internationalism, individualism and socialism in their writing. They drew their inspiration from ancient scriptures, *Upanisads* and *Gita*. They revived the ancient *Vedanta* philosophy in modern garb. They synthesised spiritual truths with scientific discoveries. They pleaded for a meeting of Eastern and Western culture and religion. They advocated a world government and a world state, so that humanity may march in its onward progress as one solid community. They reconciled modern activities with ancient ideals of renunciation. Thus in metaphysics, epistemology, psychology, ethics, religion, education, social and political sciences, Sri Aurobindo, Tagore, Vivekananda, Gandhi and Radhakrishnan have maintained eclectic approach, the only proper perspective for the future speculative activity of man.

Idealism

According to Adams, "Idealism in one form or other permeates the whole of the history of philosophy."[8] This is particularly true in the case of Indian philosophy and with special reference to Indian philosophy of education. Explaining the idealist philosophy of education, Rusk said, "It bestows dignity and grandeur upon human life by emphasising the distinctiveness of man's nature, attributing to him powers, not possessed by animals, which issue in ideal—logical and aesthetic; it admits the existence of a Supreme Being; by its respect for human personality it provides the basis for democracy."[9] Except J.L. Nehru and M.N. Roy whose metaphysics may be called scientific naturalism, all the other notable Indian philosophers of education followed *Neo-vedanta* philosophy, a contemporary version of ancient Indian idealism. Therefore, they presented a teleological explanation of the world with harmony between man and Nature. They provided central place to man in the universe and presented axiological explanation of the world enigma. According to them, ideas and ideals are the aims of education. This idealist trend, however, was not opposed to realism, positivism and pragmatism. Therefore, a synthesis between all these is possible.

Realism

The philosophy of realism is almost opposed to that of idealism. According to the realist the world is material in nature and the object and its qualities exist outside the mind and without any necessary relation with it. Thus realist metaphysics is materialism, epistemology positivism and axiology pragmatism. In contemporary Indian philosophy of education, however, one finds a meeting of the extremes of idealism and realism. This is due to their eclectic and integral approach to thought and life. This meeting of extremes may be found in the educational philosophy of Vivekananda, Dayananda, Sri Aurobindo, Rabindra Nath Tagore, Gandhi and Radhakrishnan. In the aims and ideals of education they were idealists while their detailed plans of education were based upon realism and pragmatism.

Pragmatism

Pragmatism believes that man's first concern is to make this world worthy of human life. Pragmatism is this worldly. It is against all other-worldly goals. It is pluralistic. It is utilitarian. It lays emphasis upon change as a necessary element of life. It is individualist though emphasising the social aspect of man. It is humanist and experimentalist. In the field of education, therefore, the pragmatist trend has led to emphasis upon economic, cultural and ethical progress of the individuals so that they may develop characters of world-citizens. This is a sound basis for the creation of a better world in future. Programmes and schemes for social service at different stages of education today find an important place in educational institutions. The boys and girls, from time-to-time, render social service to the community outside the educational institutions so that they may develop a habit of genuine altruism and social service. This social service is based upon the value of equality of all human beings.

Contemporary Indian philosophy of education has to be pragmatist since its avowed aim was to present a national system of education suitable for a free country. These philosophers were very much conversant with the socio-economic problems of Indian masses, their poverty and illiteracy. Therefore, while drawing the details of their schemes of education they have everywhere paid attention to making education a means of livelihood while being a means of integral development of human personality. The pragmatic approach is explicit in the advice of Vivekananda to the students to care more for body building than even spiritual development. M.K. Gandhi's scheme of basic education was everywhere guided by pragmatic spirit.

A Possible Synthesis

An Ideal Philosophy of Education for Today

From the critical evaluation and systematic understanding of the educational philosophy of Swami Vivekananda, Sri Aurobindo, Swami Dayananda, M.K. Gandhi, Rabindra Nath Tagore, Sarvapalli Radhakrishnan, J.L. Nehru and M.N. Roy, it is clear that a synthesis of the prominent trends is possible. Such a synthesis will lay down the outline of an ideal philosophy of education for today. It is difficult to draw such an outline in details. However, it should be remembered that integral humanism may be called an ideal philosophy of education which may synthesis the contemporary trends in education discussed in this chapter so far. The following points emerge from the attempt of a possible synthesis:

1. Integral Aim of Education

There is the general agreement among the Indian philosophers of education that the aim of education must be integral. The educator should keep in his mind all the aspects of education, the educand and the educator. The more comprehensive and integral the aim of education the better it is for the human beings. Thus, education should aim at all round development of all the educands without distinction of caste, creed, race, sex, social or economic status, etc.

2. Integral Psychology

Indian philosophers have given an all round and integral picture of human nature. Man must be seen from every perspective and it should be remembered that each element in his nature has a right for full freedom and development. Not only the rational but also the infra-rational and the supra-rational aspects of human nature must find a place in a humanist scheme of education. While man has a soul he has also a body, a mind and an intellect and, therefore, education must provide opportunities and facilities for the fullest development of all these different aspects of man.

3. Wide Based Curriculum

Contemporary education can be humanised in so far as we provide for a wide based curriculum. There should be teaching of science, arts, literature, technology along with moral, religious and spiritual teaching. Thus, no aspect of man's development should be left out of the curriculum. Our contemporary philosophers of education have not only accepted the value of sense training and physical education along with academic, moral and religious education, but emphasised it as necessary for the all round development of the educands.

4. Mother Tongue as Medium of Instruction

Humanism and internationalism do not contradict nationalism or narrower loyalties but in fact fulfill them. The wider the circle of human relationships the more it fulfills the narrow circle and does not contradict it. Therefore, the education everywhere should fulfill local needs. The best medium of the early education of the child is the mother tongue. In the absence of education through mother tongue no originality can be developed among the educands. Keeping this importance of the mother tongue, our contemporary philosophers of education have unanimously supported the need of early education through mother tongue.

They have also emphasized the need of the growth of a national language along with the local dialect. None of them was against the study of foreign languages, in fact most of them were themselves well versed in several languages and supported their deep study but the primary and most important position was always given to mother tongue and national language.

5. Democratic School Management

Humanist culture is democratic culture. In order to be a humanist one must know how to live democratically; this is possible only if right from the childhood he is given a democratic environment. The educational institutions, should be therefore organised on democratic pattern. In this pattern the educators and the educands will participate in all the aspects of school management, formulation of curriculum, teaching methods, extra-curricular activities, etc. The educational institution should be a community absolutely democratic so that its members may develop democratic values.

6. Synthesis of Nationalism and Internationalism

Humanism stands for internationalism. This, however, does not mean that it is against nationalism. Only a narrow nationalism is anti-humanist, otherwise sound and healthy nationalism everywhere fulfils the humanist aim of the growth of a rich human culture. In the community of human culture, each nation has to contribute its share through its own culture. Therefore, in order to develop a humanist culture upon the earth, each nation should encourage the humanist elements in its culture and present them in indigenous forms. This synthesis of the national and international ideals should be developed through educational institutions. Our contemporary Indian philosophers of education were born in an age of the rise of national spirit in India. They worshipped the nation and yet in a true humanist spirit they everywhere supported international contact and co-operation. The universities at Santiniketan and Pondicherry bear testimony to this fact.

In the end it should be remembered that in order to humanize contemporary education, the humanist values should be given the most prominent place in every field of education, aims, agencies, curriculum, teacher's training, teaching methods and techniques, school management and evaluation and measurement, etc. Everywhere the all round development of each educand should be the aim of the educator. To achieve this circumstances should be created in which the educators may also develop humane character and high human values. It is only then that they can present examples before the educands. Indian philosophers have laid emphasis upon spiritual values in human life. These spiritual values make men characteristically humane. Therefore, these values must find place in our scheme of humanization of contemporary education. The suggestions advanced by our contemporary Indian philosophers of education, including Sri Aurobindo, Swami Vivekananda, Rabindra Nath Tagore, M.K. Gandhi and Swami Dayananda will be most useful for formulating such a scheme of national education.

It can be said without exaggeration that the philosophy of education maintained by these philosophers alone can supply the fundamentals for a humanist education in India.

References

1. Aurobindo, S. *The Renaissance in India*, p. 72.
2. Radhakrishnan, S., *An Idealist View of Life*, p. 205.
3. Bhagwan Das, *The Science of the Self*, p. 44.
4. *Ibid.*, p. 137 footnote.
5. Radhakrishnan, S., *An Idealist View of Life.*, p. 142.
6. Aurobindo, S., *Integral Education*, compiled by Dr. Indra Sen, p. 4.
7. Aurobindo, S., *The Life Divine*, Vol. II, p. 726.
8. Adams, Sir John, *The Evolution of Educational Theory*, p. 28.
9. Rusk, R. R., *The Philosophical Bases of Education*, p. 154.

Bibliography

Original Sources

Aurobindo, S., *The Life Divine*, Vol. II, Second Edition, (Pondicherry: Sri Aurobindo Ashram).

—, *The Life Divine* New York: (The Sri Aurobindo Library Inc., 1951).

—, *Essay on the Gita (Complete)*, Second Series (Calcutta: Arya Publishing House, 1949).

—, *Essays on the Gita (Complete)*, (New York: The Sri Aurobindo Library Inc., 1950).

—, *The Human Cycle* (New York: The Sri Aurobindo Library, Inc., 1950).

—, *The Synthesis of Yoga*, 1st University Edition (Pondicherry: Sri Aurobindo Ashram).

—, *The Synthesis of Yoga (Complete)*, (New York: The Sri Aurobindo Library, Inc., 1950).

—, *The Foundations of Indian Culture* (Pondicherry: Sri Aurobindo Ashram, 1959).

—, *Letters of Sri Aurobindo, First Series* (Bombay: Sri Aurobindo Circle, 1950).

—, *Letters of Sri Aurobindo, Second Series.*

—, *Letters of Sri Aurobindo, Third Series.*

—, *Letters of Sri Aurobindo, Fourth Series.*

— , *Supramental Manifestation* (Pondicherry: Sri Aurobindo Ashram, 1952).

—, *The Ideal of Karmayogin* (Calcutta: Arya Publishing House, 1945).

—, *The Renaissance in India* (Pondicherry: Sri Aurobindo Ashram, 1951).

—, *The Doctrine of Passive Resistance* (Culcutta: Arya Publishing House, 1948).

Aurobindo, S., *The Riddle of This World* (Pondicherry: Sri Aurobindo Ashram, 1945).

—, *After the War* (Pondicherry: Sri Aurobindo Ashram, 1949).

—, *On Nationalism* (Pondicherry: Sri Aurobindo Ashram, 1965).

—, *On India: A Compilation* (Pondicherry: Sri Aurobindo Ashram, 1957).

—, *Science and Culture* (Pondicherry: Sri Aurobindo Ashram,

—, *Uttar Para Speech*, 5th Ed. (Pondicherry: Sri Aurobindo Ashram, 1950).

—, *Unity and War and Self-Determination* (Pondicherry: Sri Aurobindo Ashram, 1962).

—, *Sri Aurobindo on Future of India* (Pondicherry: Sri Aurobindo Ashram, 1955).

—, *The Spirit and Form of Indian Polity* (Calcutta: Arya Publishing House, 1947).

—, *Bankim-Tilak-Dayananda*, 3rd Edition (Pondicherry: Sri Aurobindo Ashram, 1955).

—, *Social and Political Thought* (Pondicherry: Sri Aurobindo British Centenary Lib., 1970).

—, *Heraclitus*, 2nd Edition (1947).

—, *A System of National Education* (Calcutta: Arya Publishing House, 1949).

—, *The Mother* (Calcutta: Arya Sahitya Bhawan, 1928).

—, *Bases of Yoga*, (Pondicherry: Sri Aurobindo Ashram, 1952).

—, *Evolution*, (Calcutta: Arya Publishing House, 1944).

—, *Lights on Yoga* (Pondicherry: Sri Aurobindo Ashram, 1953).

—, *Thoughts and Aphorisms* (Pondicherry: Sri Aurobindo Ashram, 1958).

—, "Ancient India," *Indian Review*, 38 (1937).

Aurobindo, S., "Aurobindo's Political Testament", *Indian Review, 21* (1920).

—, "Indian Nationalism", *Advent*, 24 (4) (Nov. 1967)

—, "The New Society", *Sri Aurobindo Circle*, No. XVI (1960).

—, "Task Before New India", *Bhavaris Journal* 3 (2) (April 1965).

—, "The Vitality of Hindu Culture", *Indian Review*, 21 (1920).

Dayananda, S., *Satyartha Prakash*, English translation by Dr. Chiranjiva Bharadwaja, (New Delhi: Sarvadeshik Arya Pratinidhi Sabha, 1975).

Gandhi, M.K., *An Autobiography or The Story of My Experiments with Truth,* Translation by Mahadev Desai, 2 Vols. (Ahmedabad: Navajivan Press, 1927 & 1929).

—, *Bapu's Letters to Mira* (Ahmedabad: 1949).

—, *Christian Missions* (Ahmedabad: 1949).

—, *Communal Unity,* (Ahmedabad: 1949).

—, *Conquest of Self,* Edited by R.K. Prabhu and U.R. Rao, (Bombay: 1943).

—, *Constructive Programme* (Ahmedabad: 1941).

—, *Daridranarayana,* Edited by A.T. Hingorani (Karachi: 1946).

—, *Delhi Diary* (Ahmedabad: 1948).

—, *Economics of Khadi,* (Ahmedabad: 1941).

—, *Ethical Religion* (Madras: 1922).

—, *For Pacifists* (Ahmedabad: 1949).

—, *From Yeravadu Mandir* (Ahmedabad: 1933).

—, Gandhij's Correspondence with the Government: 1942-1944, (Ahmedabad: 1945).

—, *Harijan* (1933-1940), (1942), (1946-1950).

—, *Hind Swaraj,* (Madras: Natesan, 1921).

—, *Hind Swaraj* (Ahmedabad: 1948).

—, Indian States Problem (Ahmedabad: 1941).

Gandhi, M.K., *Key to Health* (Ahmedabad: 1948).

—, *The Mind of Mahatma Gandhi*, Edited by R.K. Prabhu & U.R. Rao (Bombay: 1945).

—, *My Appeal to the British*, Edited by A.T. Hingorani, (Karachi: 1942).

—, *My Soul's Agony* (Bombay: 1932).

—, *Non-Violence in Peace and War*, 2 Vols. (Ahmedabad: 1942 & 1949).

—, *Our Language Problem*, Edited by A.T. Hingorani (Lucknow: Poona Statements, 1933).

—, *Satyagraha Ashram Ka Itihas,* Translated by R.N. Chowdhary (Ahmedabad: 1948).

—, *Satyagraha in South Africa* (Madras: 1928).

—, *Satyagraha in South Africa* (Ahmedabad: 1950).

—, *Selections from Gandhi* Edited by N.K. Bose, (Ahmedabad: 1948).

—, *Self-Restraint* versus *Self-Indulgence,* 2 Parts, (Ahmedabad: 1930 & 1939).

—, Speeches and Writings of M.K. Gandhi *(Madras: 1922).*

—, *To the Princes and Their People,* Edited by A.T. Hingorani (Karachi: 1942).

—, *To the Students* (Ahmedabad: 1949).

—, *To the Women,* Edited by A.T. Hingorani (Karachi: 1945).

—, *The Wheel of Fortune* (Madras: 1922).

—, *Women and Social Injustice* (Ahmedabad: 1942).

—, *Young India (Weekly),* (1919-1932).

—, *Young India (Selections),* I, (1919-1922); II, (1924-1926); III, (1927-1928), (Madras).

Nehru, J.L., *An Autobiography : With Musings on India* (New Delhi: Allied Publishers Pvt. Ltd., 1962).

—, *A Bunch of Old Letters* (Bombay: Asia Publishing House, 1958).

—, *China, Spain and the War: Essays and Writings* (Allahabad: Kitabistan, 1940).

Nehru, J.L., *Eighteen Months in India: Being Further Essays and Writings, 1936-1937* (Allahabad: Kitabistan, 1938).

—, *Glimpses of World History,* 2nd Edn. in one Vol. (Bombay: Asia Publishing House, 1962).

—, *Independence and After: A Collection of Speeches, 1946- 1949,* (New Delhi: Publication Division, Government of India, 1949).

—, "On Community Development", *Indian National Congress* (1949).

—, *India and The World: Essays,* (London: George Allen and Unwin Ltd., 1936).

—, *India Today and Tomorrow: Azad Memorial Lectures* (New Delhi: Indian Council of Cultural Relations, 1959).

—, *Letters from a Father to His Father* (London: Oxford University Press, 1964).

—, *Mahatma Gandhi* (Calcutta: Signet Press, 1949).

—, *Communalism and other Subjects* (Allahabad: May, 1934).

—, *Socialism by Consent* (Alipore: Publicity Deptt., West Bengal Govt. Press, 1957).

—, *Soviet Russia: Some Random Sketches and Impressions,* Reprinted (Bombay : Chetna, 1949).

—, *The Discovery of India* (Bombay: Asia Publishing House, 1964).

—, *The Unity of India: Collected Writings 1937-1940,* London: Lindsay Drummound, 1948).

—, *Visit to America* (New York: John Day Co., 1950).

—, *Selected Speeches and Writings*, (New Delhi: Perspective Publications Pvt. Ltd., 1964).

Radhakrishnan, S., *An Idealist View of Life* (London: George Allen & Unwin, 1947).

—, *The Hindu Views of Life* (London: George Allen & Unwin, 1961).

— , *The Concept of Man* (London: George Allen & Unwin, 1960).

Radhakrishnan S., *Kalki or The Future of Civilization*, 6th Edn. (Ludhiana: Kalyani Publishers, 1974).

—, *Freedom and Culture (A Collection)* (Madras: G.A. Nateson & Co., 1932).

—, *Fast and West in Religion* (London: George Allen & Unwin, 1933).

—, *The Reign of Religion in Contemporary Thought* (London: Macmillan, 1920).

—, *The Philosophy of Rabindra Nath Tagore* (Baroda: Good Companions, 1961).

—, *On Nehru* (New Delhi: Publications Division, Govt. of India, 1955).

—, *Indian Philosophy*, Vol. I, Revised Edn. (London: George Allen & Unwin, 1929).

—, *Indian Philosophy*, Vol. II, Revised Edn. (London: George Allen & Unwin, 1931).

Roy, M.N., *Science and Philosophy* (Calcutta: Renaissance Publishers, 1947).

—, *Politics, Power and Parties.*

—, *Reason, Romanticism and Revolution,* Vol. I.

—, *Radical Humanism.*

—, *New Humanism* (Calcutta: Renaissance Publishers, 1961).

Tagore, R.N., *The Post Office* (Church Town: Guala Press, 1914).

—, *Stray Birds* (London: Macmillan, 1917).

—, *Greater India* (Madras: S. Ganeshan, 1921).

—, *Talks in China* (Santiniketan: Visva-Bharati, 1925).

—, *Creative Unity* (London: Macmillan, 1925).

—, *A Poet's School*, Visva-Bharati Bulletin No. 9 (1928).

—, *City and Village*, Visva-Bharati Bulletin No. 10, (1928).

—, *The Religion of Man* (London: George Allen & Unwin, 1932).

—, *Chandalika* (1933).

Tagore, R.N., *My Boyhood Days* (Visva-Bharati, 1940).

—, *Crisis in Civilization* (Visva-Bharati, 1941).

—, *Two Sisters* (Visva-Bharati, 1945).

—, *Home and the World* (London: Macmillan, 1948).

—, *Nationalism* (London: Macmillan, 1950).

—, *Personality* (London: Macmillan, 1954).

—, *Lectures and Addresses*, Selected by Anthony, (London: Macmillan, 1955).

—, *Letters from Russia* (Visva-Bharati, 1962).

—, *Reminiscences* (London: Macmillan, 1961).

—, *Towards Universal Man* (Asia Publications, 1961).

—, *Gitanjali* (London: Macmillan, 1962).

—, *A Vision of India's History* (Visva-Bharati, 1962).

—, *The Centre of Indian Culture* (Visva-Bharati, 1962).

—, *Red Gleanders* (London: Macmillan, 1962).

—, *Gora* (London: Macmillan, 1963).

—, *The Wreck* (London: Macmillan, 1963).

—, *The Co-operative Principle* (Visva-Bharati, (1963).

—, *Sadhana* (London: Macmillan, 1963).

—, *Boundless Sky* (Visva-Bharati, 1964).

—, *A Tagore Testament* (Bombay: Jaico Publishing House, 1963).

—, *Lipika (*Bombay: Jaico Publishing House, 1969).

—, *Our Universe* (Bombay: Jaico Publishing House, 1969).

Vivekananda, S., *The Complete Works*, Vols. I-VIII (Almora: Advaita Ashram, 1947).

—, *Hinduism* (Mylapore: Sri Ramkrishna Math).

—, *Our Women* (Almora: Advaita Ashram).

—, *Lectures from Colombo to Almora* (Almora: Advaita Ashram).

—, *To the Youth of India* (Almora: Advaita Ashram).

—, *Almora Thoughts of Powers* (Almora: Advaita Ashram).

Secondary Sources

Abhenanda, S., *Ideal of Education* (Calcutta: Ramkrishna Vedanta Math, 1945).

—, Swami Vivekananda and His Works in America *(Almora: Advaita Ashram, 1939).*

Adams, Sir John, *The Evolution of Educational Theory,* (London: Macmillan, 1912).

Agrawal, R.S., *Mind and Vision* (1978).

Agrawal, S.N., *The Gandhian Plan* (Bombay: Padama Publications, 1944).

Altekar, A.S., *Education in Ancient India* (Banaras: Indian Bookshop, 1934).

Andrews, C.F., *Mahatma Gandhi's Ideas* (London: George Allen & Unwin, 1929).

Arapura, J.G., *Radhakrishnan and Integral Experience* (Bombay: Asia Publishing House, 1966).

Barret, C., *Philosophy* (New York: Macmillan, 1935).

Basu, A.N., "Tagore's Educational Philosophy in Relation to Basic Education", *Visva-Bharati Quarterly,* Education Number (1947).

Bhattacharya, K., "Rabindra Nath on Religion", *Homage from Visva-Bharati* (1962).

Bhattacharya, A.C., *Sri Aurobindo and Bergson* (Gyanpur: Jaga Bandhu Prakashan, 1972).

Bhattacharya, P.K., *A Scheme of Education* (Pondicherry: Sri Aurobindo Ashram, 1952).

Blanshard and others, *Philosophy in American Education* (New York: Harper & Brothers, 1945).

Broudy, J.S., *Building a Philosophy of Education* (Englewood Cliffs: N.J. Prentice-Hall, 1961).

Bruner, J.S., *The Process of Education* (Harvard University Press, 1960).

Cohn, S.M., *The Philosophical Foundation of Education* (New York: Harper & Row Publishers, 1970).

Cole, G.D.H., *Essays in Social Theory* (London: Macmillan, 1950).

Cunningham, J.W., *Problems of Philosophy* (Calcutta: Chakravartty, Chatterjee & Co , 1957).

Datta, D.M., *The Philosophy of Mahatma Gandhi* (Canada: University of Wisconsin Press, 1953).

Dewey, John, *Democracy and Education* (New York: Macmillan, 1916).

Dowsett, N.C., *The Psychology for Future Education* (Pondicherry: Sri Aurobindo Ashram, 1977).

Ducasse, C.J., *Philosophy of Art* (New York: Dial Press, 1926).

Fischer, Louis, *A Week with Gandhi* (New York: Duel Sloan and Pearce, 1942).

—, *The Life of Mahatma Gandhi* (New York: Harper & Brothers, 1950).

Gregg, R.B., *Gandhism and Socialism* (Madras: Ganesan, 1931).

Grumber, F.C., *Foundations for a Philosophy of Education* (New York: Crowell-Collier Publishing Co., 1961).

Hampton, H.V., *The Educational System* (London: Oxford University Press, 1943).

Hughes, A.G., *Education and the Democratic Ideal* (London: Longman's Green & Co., 1951).

Huxley, A., *Ends and Means* (London: Chatto & Windus, 1951).

Joshi, K., *Nav Chetna* (New Delhi: Mothers International School, 1977).

Kane, P.V., *History of Dharmasastras*, Vol. II (Pune: Bhandarkar Oriental Research Institute, 1941).

Kilpatrick, W.H., *Source Book in the Philosophy of Education* (New York: Macmillan, 1934).

Kumarappa, J.C., *Education for Life* (Rajamundry: Hindustan. Publishing Co., 1937).

Lamont, C., *The Philosophy of Hinduism* (London: Vision Press Ltd., 1962).

Mahadevan, T.M.P. & G.V. Saroja, *Contemporary Indian Philosophy* (New Delhi: Sterling Publishers, 1981).

Maitra, S.K., The Meeting of the East and the West in Sri Aurobindo's Philosophy *(Pondicherry: Sri Aurobindo Ashram, 1956).*

—, *History of the Future* (Pondicherry: Sri Aurobindo Ashram, 1956).

—, Sri Aurobindo Mandir Annual, Vol. II.

Mani, R.S., *Educational Ideas and Ideals of Gandhi and Tagore* (New Delhi: New Book Society of India, November 1965).

Patel, M.S., *The Educational Philosophy of Mahatma Gandhi* (Ahmedabad: Navajivan Publishing House, 1953).

Pillai, N.P., *The Educational Aims of Mahatma Gandhi*, (Trivandrum: Kalyanmandir Publications, 1959).

Prakash, S., *A Critical Study of Philosophy of Dayananda*, (Ajmer: Vedic Pustakalaya, 1938).

Ramkrishna, S., *For Thinkers on Education* (Madras: Sri Ramkrishna Math, 1948).

Roy, S., *The Restless Brahmin: Early Life of M.N. Roy* (New Delhi: Allied Publishers Private Ltd.).

Roy, Wood & Sellers, *The Principles and Problems of Philosophy* (New York: Macmillan, 1926).

Robert, R.R., *The Philosophical Bases of Education* (London: University of London Press, 1956).

Rousseau, J.J., *Emile* (London: J.M. Dent & Sons, 1950).

Sarma, D.S., *Studies in Renaissance of Hinduism* (Banaras: Banaras Hindu University, 1944).

Schilpp, P.A., *The Philosophy of Sarvapalli Radhakrishnan* (Tudor Publishing House, 1952).

Sellers, R.W., *The Principles and Problems of Philosophy* (New York: Macmillan, 1926).

Sen, Indra, *The Message and Mission of Indian Culture* (Pondicherry: Sri Aurobindo Ashram, 1951).

Sethna, K.D., *The Indian Spirit and the World Future* (Pondicherry: Sri Aurobindo Ashram, 1953).

Sharma, R.N., *Problems of Philosophy* (Meerut: KNRN, 1982).

Sharma, R.N. *Indian Philosophy* (New Delhi: Orient Longman's Ltd., 1972).

—, *Social Philosophy of Sri Aurobindo* (Meerut: Vineet, 1979).

—, *Philosophy of Sri Aurobindo* (Meerut: KNRN, 1972).

—, *Educational Philosophy of Sri Aurobindo* (Agra: Vinod Pustak Mandir, 1985).

—, "Sri Aurobindo's Integral Method in Philosophy", *Agra University Journal of Research (Letters)*, Vol. XI, Part II (1964).

—, "Control of Psi Phenomena in Sri Aurobindo's Yoga", *Indian Journal of Parapsychology*, Vol. III, No. 4 (1961-1962).

Shrimali, K.L., *The Wardha Scheme of Education* (Udaipur: Vidyabhavan Society, 1949).

Tagore, S., *Rabindra Nath Tagore and Universal Humanism* (Bombay: Standard Vacuum Oil Company, 1961).

Upadhyaya, G.P., *The Origin, Scope and Mission of Arya Samaj* (Ahmedabad: 1940).

Vishwa Prakash, *Life and Teachings of Swami Dayananda* (Allahabad: 1935).

Vyas, K.C., *The Social Renaissance in India* (Bombay: Vora & Co. Pvt. Ltd., 1957).

William Cenkner, The Hindu Personality in Education (*Tagore, Gandhi and Aurobindo*) (Manohar, 1976).